Intelligent Guides

MW01282339

Bordeaux: Right Bank

August 2018 edition

Benjamin Lewin MW
Copyright © 2015, 2016, 2017, 2018 Benjamin Lewin
ISBN 978-1976938610
Vendange Press
www.vendangepress.com

Preface

This Guide is devoted specifically to the Right Bank of Bordeaux, including St. Emilion, Pomerol, their satellite appellations, and the Côtes de Bordeaux. The Left Bank is discussed in a separate guide, which includes the Médoc, Graves, and Sauternes. The first part of the guide discusses the regions and explains the character and range of the wines. The second part profiles the producers. There are detailed profiles of the leading producers, showing how each winemaker interprets the local character, and mini-profiles of other important estates.

In the first part, I address the nature of the wines made today and ask how this has changed, how it's driven by tradition or competition, and how styles may evolve in the future. I show how the wines are related to the terroir and to the types of grape varieties that are grown, and I explain the classification system. For each region, I suggest reference wines that illustrate the character and variety of the area.

In the second part, there's no single definition for what constitutes a top producer. Leading châteaux range from those who are so prominent as to represent the common public face of an appellation to those who demonstrate an unexpected potential on a tiny scale. The châteaux profiled in the guide represent the best of both tradition and innovation in wine in the region. In each profile, I have tried to give a sense of the producer's aims for his wines, of the personality and philosophy behind them—to meet the person who makes the wine, as it were, as much as to review the wines themselves.

Each profile shows a sample label, a picture of the winery, and details of production, followed by a description of the producer and winemaker. Each producer is rated (from one to four stars). For each producer I suggest reference wines that are a good starting point for understanding the style. Most of the producers welcome visits, although some require appointments: details are in the profiles. Profiles are organized geographically, and are preceded by maps showing the locations of châteaux to help plan itineraries.

The guide is based on many visits to Bordeaux over recent years. I owe an enormous debt to the châteaux who cooperated in this venture by engaging in discussion and opening innumerable bottles for tasting. This guide would not have been possible without them.

Benjamin Lewin

Contents

Tables

Appellation Maps

Producer Maps

Overview of the Right Bank

Bordeaux is really two regions, divided by the Garonne river and its continuation into the Gironde estuary. The city of Bordeaux is on the left bank, which includes the Médoc to the north of the city, and the Graves to the south. On the other side of the river, the right bank includes all of the appellations extending to the east. These vary from the lowest in the hierarchy, the AOP Bordeaux, to the heights of St. Emilion and Pomerol.

Around three quarters of Bordeaux comes from the right bank. The majority of producers are on the right bank; more than half make wines only of the Bordeaux and the Côtes de Bordeaux appellations. The estates tend to be smaller on the right bank than the left bank, and this is where many of the "petit châteaux" are located: essentially small producers. (Château is essentially a synonym for wine producer in Bordeaux: on the right bank, most of the "châteaux" are perfectly ordinary, workmanlike buildings.) Much of the material for Bordeaux brands is sourced from the right bank.

The right bank is a land of extremes: on the one hand, some of the most expensive wines in Bordeaux come from Pomerol and St. Emilion; on the other, producers of generic AOP Bordeaux cannot get back the costs of production from the sale of a bottle. Whereas the wines of the petit châteaux can be on the thin side, those of St. Emilion and Pomerol are the most generous in Bordeaux. Most producers are conventional châteaux, but the right bank is the home of Bordeaux's boutique wines, known locally as garage wines.

If it were not for the history of concentrating distribution through the city of Bordeaux, the right bank might well have been defined as a different region from the left bank. It shares the same principle of assemblage from more than one variety, but the principal grape is Merlot, and often the only other variety is Cabernet Franc, whereas the left bank is famous for its Cabernet Sauvignon. Its appearance is different, with gently rolling hills rather than the flatness of the Médoc or Graves. Going around the châteaux feels like navigating through a rabbit warren, compared with the linearity of the Médoc. Whereas the left bank was famous by the eighteenth century, the right bank developed more recently, coming to fame only in the second half of the twentieth century.

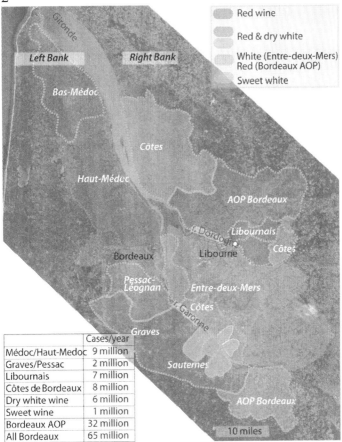

	Cases/year
Médoc/Haut-Medoc	9 million
Graves/Pessac	2 million
Libournais	7 million
Côtes de Bordeaux	8 million
Dry white wine	6 million
Sweet wine	1 million
Bordeaux AOP	32 million
All Bordeaux	65 million

The left bank is to the west of the Garonne and the right bank is to the east. Most of the right bank is AOP Bordeaux, Côtes de Bordeaux, or Entre-deux-Mers, all producing both red and white wine. A cluster of appellations in the Libournais produce only red wine.

The Appellations

Virtually all wine in Bordeaux falls under the Appellation Contrôlée system. Accounting for about half of all production, AOP Bordeaux is the lowest level of the hierarchy. It can come from anywhere in the Bordeaux region, but most of the areas that produce wine for this generic level are on the right bank.

At the next level up, there are some broad district appellations. Côtes de Bordeaux describes wine coming from several regions. The major areas are adjacent to the river on the right bank; other areas are at the northeastern edge of the Bordeaux region. Each area can append its own name to Côtes de Bordeaux (Blaye, Cadillac, Castillon, Francs). Côte de Bourg is a separate area adjacent to Côtes de Bordeaux Blaye, at the northern end of the right bank.

Entre-deux-Mers (which literally means "between two seas") describes the region between the Garonne and Dordogne rivers. The areas of the Côtes and Entre-deux-Mers produce red and white wines (although red wine produced in Entre-deux-Mers is labeled as AOP Bordeaux).

Premières Côtes de Bordeaux is a small area adjacent to the Garonne on the right bank, and covers the areas for sweet wine production that face the better known area of Sauternes across the river.

The most important appellations on the right bank are the Libournais, a small cluster of appellations taking their name from the town of Libourne on the Dordogne river (formerly a port for exporting wine). The best appellations in the Libournais are St. Emilion and Pomerol, surrounded by a group of satellite appellations, often taking names that play off their more famous cousins, such as Montagne St. Emilion and Lalande-de-Pomerol. They produce only red wine. To the east of the Libournais, the Côtes de Bordeaux Castillon is similar to the satellites, but less well known.

Another fifty miles to the east of Bordeaux, the appellations of the Dordogne make red and both dry and sweet white wines from similar blends to Bordeaux (see *Guide to Wines of Southwest France*).

The Grape Varieties

The rules allow the same grape varieties to be grown anywhere in Bordeaux, but Merlot and Cabernet Franc dominate the right bank, compared to Cabernet Sauvignon and Merlot on the left bank. The clay-based soils of the right bank are cooler than the gravel-based soils of the left bank, and so require varieties that ripen more easily.

The right bank is three quarters Merlot. The remaining quarter is Cabernet, mostly Cabernet Franc. There is some Cabernet Sauvignon; this is at its lowest in the Libournais, where it is rarely above 10%.

The key to understanding the style(s) of Bordeaux is blending, but this is not so variable on the right bank as on the left bank. Most right bank wines are blends between a majority of Merlot and a minority of Cabernet Franc. The blend does not change greatly from year to year.

It's often more than 80% Merlot in Pomerol, and a bit less in St. Emilion, but there are some monovarietal Merlots.

The dominance of Merlot gives right bank wines their generosity, even overt fruitiness. As a minor partner, Cabernet Franc adds structure and freshness to lighten up the Merlot, bringing some restraint, sometimes with a leafy, tobacco quality. Because Merlot develops more sugar at ripeness than Cabernet Sauvignon, right bank wines tend to be higher in alcohol, often a percent more than their left bank equivalents.

Differences in the times at which each variety reaches ripeness are partly responsible for vintages in which one bank does better than the other. The usual order of picking starts with Merlot in Graves and Pomerol, then Merlot in St. Emilion, then the Cabernets on the left and right banks. When the weather changes between picking the Merlot and Cabernets, it can create a significant difference between right bank wines based on Merlot and left bank wines based on Cabernet.

White wine comes from a blend of Sauvignon Blanc and Sémillon, the traditional proportions being 80% and 20%, although there are now some 100% Sauvignon Blancs. This is the same blend as for white Graves of the left bank.

The Libournais

The heart of quality on the right bank is the Libournais. The border between the top appellations, St. Emilion and Pomerol, is all but imperceptible. Pomerol is the epitome of Merlot, as flaunted by its top château, Petrus, which is effectively a monovarietal. The focus on Merlot brings a general style that is lush, full, and fruity—more so in Pomerol than in St. Emilion, because there is usually less Cabernet Franc in Pomerol. There is more clay in the soil in Pomerol, which suits Merlot best, and more limestone in St. Emilion, which favors Cabernet Franc.

The dividing line can seem a bit arbitrary if you compare the châteaux on the Pomerol side of the border with their neighbors in St. Emilion. From Château Cheval Blanc, vineyards run continuously across the plateau to the church at Pomerol, surrounded by a group of the top Pomerol châteaux. In any case, the difference in style has narrowed a bit in the past decade with the move to increased ripeness.

The satellite appellations form an arc around Pomerol and St. Emilion. Fronsac and Canon-Fronsac lie to the west, and Lalande de Pomerol is just north of Pomerol. Various subsidiary St. Emilion appel-

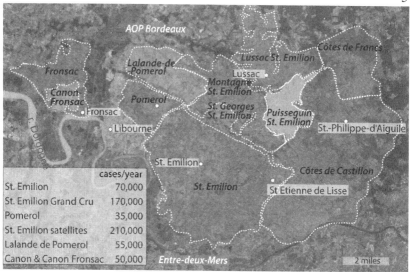

	cases/year
St. Emilion	70,000
St. Emilion Grand Cru	170,000
Pomerol	35,000
St. Emilion satellites	210,000
Lalande de Pomerol	55,000
Canon & Canon Fronsac	50,000

St. Emilion and Pomerol are the heart of the Libournais, ringed by a series of satellite appellations. The appellations to the north are separated from St. Emilion and Pomerol by the stream of the Barbanne. To the south, across the Dordogne, is Entre-deux-Mers. To the east are the Côtes de Bordeaux Castillon and Francs.

lations to the north of St. Emilion aim for similar style, but have less intensity. To the east, Castillon has limestone terroir like St. Emilion.

St. Emilion

There is huge variation in terroirs in St. Emilion, to the point at which you wonder how on earth it could have been defined as a single AOC. The answer is that the appellation follows medieval boundaries, with no recognition of the underlying geology. The town of St. Emilion lies at the center of the appellation. Around it is a limestone plateau, where most of the top châteaux are located. This is called the *calcaire à astéries*, meaning that it's limestone embedded with fossils. Even on the limestone, there is wide variation in the depth of topsoil, but it's the wines from this part of the appellation that define St. Emilion.

The plateau is perfect terroir for Cabernet Franc (which was in fact St. Emilion's traditional variety before planting of Merlot was encouraged after phylloxera). The cooler clay and limestone soils on the plateau make for later harvests, typically a couple of weeks after the rest of the appellation. Around the limestone plateau, soils are sandy to

The town of St. Emilion is on a high point looking out over rolling vineyards.

the west and based on sandstone to the north. To the south, slopes with more alluvial soils run down to the plain bordering the Dordogne. Close to the river the classification becomes mere AOP Bordeaux.

The terroir is different in the northwest of the appellation. A gravelly area runs between St. Emilion and Pomerol. There is more Cabernet Franc here, especially at Cheval Blanc where it is usually around half the blend, and there is even some Cabernet Sauvignon at Château Figeac, where the usual blend is one third each of Cabernets Sauvignon and Franc, and Merlot. Châteaux just across the border in Pomerol also have more Cabernet Franc (and sometimes resemble St. Emilion in style, compared with their more opulent counterparts in the heart of the Pomerol).

St. Emilion has taken an unusual lead in requiring that from the 2019 vintage all viticulture has to be certified as sustainable. Acceptable methods range from the minimum of *lutte raisonnée*, which means in effect that sprays such as fungicides are used only when needed, not as a matter of routine, to fully organic methods. Herbicides have been banned entirely. Any wine made from grapes farmed by conventional methods cannot be labeled as St. Emilion, but must be labeled only as Bordeaux. The regulations also apply to the satellite appellations of Lussac St.-Emilion and Puisseguin St.-Emilion.

The average size of classified châteaux is 16 ha in St. Emilion, compared with 60 ha for the Grand Cru Classés of the Médoc. By contrast with the many grand châteaux in the Médoc, the buildings are more modest on the right bank. But this is changing. Sharp increases in the value of land have caused many family properties to be sold, not just because of inheritance taxes, but because owners in the family who are not directly involved in wine production want to cash out. The price of top vineyards has reached €2-3 million per hectare. Flying winemaker Michel Rolland was forced to sell the family estate, Château Bon Pasteur. "It was a family problem—I knew for years that I was going to have to sell the property because my brother wanted to get his share of the money out. It was sad to sell it as it's been in our family since the 1920s." The new owner is an investor from Hong Kong.

I remember when St. Emilion was a real working town. It was a bit grubby and somewhat dilapidated, but authentic. Now it's a UNESCO site, the number of inhabitants has declined from 8,000 to 2,000, and it's become a tourist site that probably holds the world record for the number of wine shops per mile. It's symbolic of the change occurring on the right bank, which used to be dominated by small family-owned estates but is now succumbing to corporate mergers and acquisitions by the owners of multiple properties, or takeovers by insurance or luxury goods companies. Some châteaux have ceased to exist as they have been incorporated into other, larger properties.

As ownership has moved more to rich individuals or corporations, the remaining family owners feel themselves squeezed out. "This is one of the remaining family estates," says Juliette Bécot at Château Beauséjour Bécot. "Family ownership was very common but now it is more and more rare. As a family estate we earn money only from viticulture, but we have to compete with owners who can invest lots of money from other sources." Michel Rolland has a pessimistic view: "No family will be able to save its patrimony."

The Grand Cru Classés

St. Emilion is the only right bank appellation to have any classification of its châteaux The best châteaux are called Grand Cru Classé. The first classification, in 1955, followed the precedent of the left bank and classified the châteaux rather than the vineyards. The original intention was to revise the classification every decade. In fact, it has been revised four times.

The criteria for classification today are a mélange of price, quality of wine, and terroir, so if a château acquires new vineyards, it may or

A sign of changing times in St. Emilion, the new winery at Cheval Blanc dwarfs the old château.

may not be allowed to use them in the classified wine. This is somewhat shutting the cellar door after the wine has been bottled, as there was never any examination of the terroirs the châteaux had at the outset when the classification was first made.

The first three revisions to the classification made relatively minor changes and were uncontroversial, but the revision in 2006 was thrown out because of legal challenges from châteaux that were demoted. A new St. Emilion classification came into effect finally in 2012. The inclusion of more properties, and the increasing size of the classified properties, has seen the proportion of Grand Cru Classé vineyards increase from 16% in 1996 to 24% in 2012.

Châteaux are divided into three classes:

- The first group is called "Premier Grand Cru Classé," the same term used for first growths in the Médoc, but is subdivided into two further groups. Originally only two châteaux were classified as the very top level of group A: Ausone and Cheval Blanc. These have always been regarded as generally equivalent to the first growths of the Médoc. Angélus and Pavie have now been promoted into this group. Group B has 14 châteaux in the latest classification. These are roughly equivalent to second growths of the Médoc.

- A further 63 châteaux are classified as Grand Cru Classés, nominally equivalent in quality to a range from classified growths of the Médoc to Cru Bourgeois. Actually, these are rather a mixed lot, and some châteaux appear to be included more in recognition of their history than for current quality.

- In addition, all the producers of St. Emilion (roughly 600 châteaux) can describe themselves as St. Emilion Grand Cru (a term which has little significance except to undermine completely the concept of "Grand Cru"). There is a world of difference between a Grand Cru Classé, which is classified, and a Grand Cru, which actually has no classification at all.

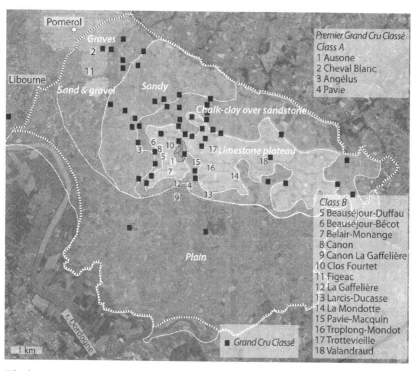

The best terroirs of St. Emilion are the limestone plateau around the town, and the Graves adjacent to Pomerol. The Premier Grand Cru Classés spread out from the town on the limestone plateau, except for Cheval Blanc and Figeac, which are on the Graves. The Grand Cru Classés are more widely dispersed. Wines from the plain are rarely in the same category.

The St. Emilion Classification of 2012	
Premier grand cru classé A	
Château Ausone	*Château Angélus*
Château Cheval Blanc	*Château Pavie*
Premier grand cru classé B	
Château Beauséjour Duffau-Lagarrosse	Château La Gaffelière
Château Beau-Séjour Bécot	*Château Larcis Ducasse*
Château Bélair-Monange	*La Mondotte*
Château Canon	*Château Pavie-Macquin*
Château Canon-la-Gaffelière	Château Troplong Mondot
Château Figeac	Château Trottevieille
Clos Fourtet	*Château Valandraud*

The reclassification provides a striking validation of the market trend to richer, more powerful, more extracted wines. Ever since the original classification, the perennial contender for promotion to group A has been Château Figeac, unusual in St. Emilion for the high content of Cabernet Sauvignon, which gives it more structure and less opulence. It had begin to seem that the very top level was inviolate, but the promotion of Angélus and Pavie really symbolizes the move in St. Emilion to a richer (and more alcoholic) style. Indeed, if the candidates for promotion had been assessed solely on the basis of ripeness *über alles*, Angélus and Pavie would have been right at the top.

Château Pavie has been controversial since a famous disagreement between critics as to whether a change in style, after Gérard Pearse bought the château in 1998, was to "a ridiculous wine more reminiscent of a late-harvest Zinfandel" (according to Jancis Robinson MW) or "an off the chart effort...trying to recreate the glories of ancient Bordeaux vintages" (according to Robert Parker). Irrespective of the merits of this wine (the 2003 vintage) the promotion is nothing if not a clear validation of the trend to power. The inclusion in the classification of the former garage wines, Valandraud and La Mondotte, as Premier Grand Cru Classé B, further reinforces the trend.

The Premier Grand Cru Classés in class B are mostly located on the limestone plateau around the town, with a large cluster just west of the town. They tend to have a little more Cabernet Franc than other wines, although the same trend to an increasing proportion of Merlot has been evident for the past few years as in the Médoc. This is partly responsible for the increased sense of richness.

Grand cru classé

Château l'Arrosée	Château Grand Pontet
Château Balestard la Tonnelle	*Château Guadet*
Château Barde-Haut	Château Haut Sarpe
Château Bellefont-Belcier	Clos des Jacobins
Château Bellevue	Couvent des Jacobins
Château Berliquet	*Château Jean Faure*
Château Cadet Bon	Château Laniote
Château Cap de Mourlin	Château Larmande
Château Chauvin	Château Laroque
Château Clos de Sarpe	Château Laroze
Château la Clotte	*Château la Madelaine*
Château la Commanderie	Château La Marzelle
Château Corbin	*Château Monbousquet*
Château Côte de Baleau	Château Moulin du Cadet
Château la Couspaude	Clos de l'Oratoire
Château Dassault	Château Pavie-Decesse
Château Destieux	Château Peby Faugères
Château la Dominique	Château Petit Faurie de Soutard
Château Faugères	*Château de Pressac*
Château Faurie de Souchard	Château Le Prieuré
Château de Ferrand	*Château Quinault l'Enclos*
Château Fleur-Cardinale	Château Ripeau
Château La Fleur Morange	*Château Rochebelle*
Château Fombrauge	Château Saint Georges (Côte Pavie)
Château Fonplégade	
Château Fonroque	Clos Saint-Martin
Château Franc Mayne	*Château Sansonnet*
Château Grand Corbin	Château La Serre
Château Grand Corbin-Despagne	Château Soutard
	Château Tertre Daugay
Château Grand Mayne	Château La Tour Figeac
Château les Grandes Murailles	Château Villemaurine
	Château Yon Figeac

Châteaux with the same classification since 1955
Châteaux promoted in 2012

The Grand Cru Classés show wide variation in quality and styles. Many are also on the limestone plateau, with most of the rest to the west; there are very few at the far east or on the plain to the south. If St.

Emilion was defined by the classified growths, it would be only about half its present size, and its terroir would be more homogeneous.

I have been struck lately by how similar the styles are for wines at the level of Grand Cru, with a general focus on superficially attractive fruits, a soft palate, and sometimes an impression almost of sweetness on the finish. This may be partly due to common reliance on a small number of oenologues; the days when each proprietor had his own style seem to have passed. "The thing that I find the most unhealthy is the lack of individuality that exists here in Bordeaux. There are around three consultants who appear to drive virtually all of the major Bordeaux players," says Jonathan Maltus of Château Teyssier.

Most of the leading châteaux in St. Emilion now produce two wines. The grand vin simply carries the name of the château. A second wine comes from a mixture of lots that are declassified because they were not successful in a certain vintage, and specific parcels that are not so good. Usually the second wine has some play on the name of the château, like Petit Cheval or Chapelle d'Ausone. Second wines tend to be more immediately approachable with less potential for aging. They are usually about a third of the price of the grand vin.

Garage Wines

The opulent style of St. Emilion became increasingly lush in the last decade of the twentieth century. "St. Emilion in the nineties was the engine for change for fine winemaking," says Jonathan Maltus. This was due to the rise of garage wines, so called because they started as very small scale production, sometimes literally in garages. The principle behind garage wines was to take tiny vineyard plots without particularly distinguished terroir, and to use extreme techniques of viticulture and vinification to produce highly extracted, concentrated wines.

There were only about five garage wines when they made their first widespread impact on the market in 1991. Then numbers increased fairly steadily until reaching a plateau a few years ago at around 30-40. Garage wines follow the principle of small is beautiful, but perhaps small is expensive would be a more appropriate description: at their peak they were the most expensive wines coming out of St. Emilion.

Garage wines have had an effect out of all proportion to their number and size. There are probably less than 200 ha of vineyards devoted to producing garage wines, generating fewer than 40,000 cases each year in total. This is not much more than the size and annual production of a single Grand Cru Classé of the Médoc. But they have moved the whole market. Initially their innovations were viewed with scorn. "In the early 1990s people in the Médoc were laughing at the garage movement in St. Emilion, but now they have adopted many of the same methods, such as green harvesting," says Stephan von Neipperg at Château Canon la Gaffelière. (Green harvesting consists of pruning off excess berries early in the season to reduce yields).

The phenomenon of garage wines was about as long lived as the wines themselves (with all that extraction they can be attractive when young but tend to fade after a decade), and many of the garagistes have moved on. The trend is typified by two wines. Château Valandraud started in 1991 with only 1,280 bottles, from vines on a relatively sandy plot of land. "I wanted to make a wine that is hedonistic and sexy, soft and chic," says Jean-Luc Thunevin, the self-styled "bad boy" of St. Emilion, who became the first garagiste when he made the first vintage of Château Valandraud (literally) in his garage. Then Valandraud acquired more and better terroirs (and a château), and in 2012 became part of the establishment when it was included in the classification.

Château La Mondotte, although sharing some of the features of garage wines, comes from a small outstanding plot of 65-year-old vines. It became a separate cuvée because the authorities would not allow it to be included in Canon-La-Gaffelière in the classification of 1996. Subsequently it achieved the reputation of a garage wine. This was the forerunner of a trend for making small cuvées from special plots. "We decided we would bring the single vineyard concept into Bordeaux," says Jonathan Maltus, who produces four special cuvées from different vineyards, pointing out that this is a natural trend for the right bank given the many small vineyards.

Some super-cuvées have been produced by segregating small vineyards of special quality from larger châteaux. Bernard Magrez is somewhat of an expert at this. Sometimes the wines remain as super-cuvées, sometimes they become independent. Magrez-Fombrauge became a separate production after starting as a selection of the best lots at Château Fombrauge. What difference does this make? "I wanted to make it clear that it's the same vines that make the wine each year. The image of a selection is not correct, it gives the impression of taking out the best each year, implying that the château isn't the top wine."

The boundaries have become blurred between garage wines, super-cuvées, and small vineyards with special terroir. There are still some garage wines fitting the original criterion of presenting super-extracted

Leading Garage Wines from St. Emilion	
La Mondotte	From 4 ha plot that the authorities refused to let Stephan von Neipperg include in Château Canon La Gaffelière. 11,000 bottles.
Le Dôme	One of four single vineyard wines made by Jonathan Maltus of Château Teyssier. Only 1.5 ha right at the town, producing 4,500 bottles.
Château Gracia	A real garage wine, coming from 3 ha plot, and made in cramped premises by Michel Gracia, formerly a stone mason. 5,000 bottles.
Château Magrez Fombrauge	Not so much a garage wine as a super-cuvée from a special plot at Château Fombrauge. 15,000 bottles.
Château Bellevue-Mondotte	Gérard Perse has used this small plot in an enclave at Pavie-Decesse to make a wine in his characteristically intense style. 4,800 bottles.
Château de Valandraud	Now classified as Grand Cru Classé with a vineyard of 14 ha to the east of St. Emilion. Now 35,000 bottles, but originally made in Jean-Luc Thunevin's garage from a much smaller plot.

character from terroir of no particular distinction, but they no longer attract the same attention. So are the garage wines finished? "As a phenomenon, that's sure. But not as a niche. But anyway, it's not the phenomenon of garage wines, it's the phenomenon of expensive wines," says Jean-Luc Thunevin.

Pomerol

Completely at the opposite extreme from the gentrified town of St. Emilion, the village of Pomerol is scarcely noticeable: the church is just about the only notable feature. All around are vineyards, mostly with domains housed in small practical buildings. Pomerol is on a small scale; the average estate is only 6-7 ha. Pomerol's most famous château, Petrus, was famous for its shabby appearance until some renovations a few years back. Coming from St. Emilion, first you cross the extension of the gravelly area, emerging onto a plateau where the

Vineyards run imperceptibly from St. Emilion into Pomerol as seen by the view at sunset from Cheval Blanc, with the church spire of Pomerol visible at the right.

top vineyards are located. This has the oldest soils, and is still relatively gravelly, with a mix of clay and limestone.

At the southeast edge of the plateau, where La Conseillante, Vieux Château Certan, Certan de May, L'Évangile, and Château Petit Village are located, Pomerol runs into St. Emilion. There tends to be more Cabernet Franc in the vineyards here, and the wines are relatively more restrained.

The most unusual soil is around Château Petrus, where an area of clay has been pushed up to the surface from lower layers. Named for its protrusion, this is the famous "buttonhole" clay that gives Petrus its unique character.

Moving from Petrus deeper into the appellation, to La Fleur Petrus, l'Église Clinet, Clinet, Latour à Pomerol, and Le Gay, there is more concentration on Merlot, which is usually between 80% and 90% of plantings, and the wines show the full-force richness of Pomerol. (Château Lafleur is an exception with its equal mix of Merlot and Cabernet Franc.)

"We have a lot of clay in the soil in Pomerol which makes it very good for us to produce Merlot, even 100% Merlot can have a lot of finesse and complexity," explains Nicolas de Bailliencourt at Château Gazin, located just the east of Petrus. (In fact, 4 ha of the Petrus vineyards belonged to Gazin until they were sold 40 years ago to pay

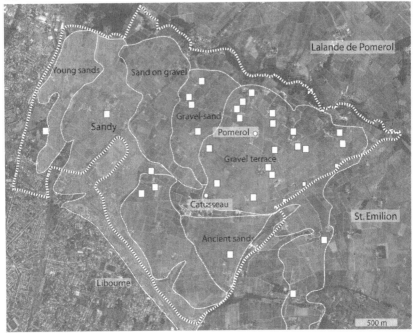

The best châteaux of Pomerol are concentrated on the plateau of gravel terraces in the northeast.

taxes. "Today one third of Petrus is made with our vines," Nicolas says ruefully.)

Although clay in the soil makes a naturally perfect terroir for Merlot, Merlot's dominance is relatively recent. It began to increase when replanting was forced by the great winter freeze of 1956. Part of today's increasingly lush style in both Pomerol and St. Emilion is due to the increase in Merlot; since 1983, it has increased in Pomerol from 65-70% to 85% today, and in St. Emilion it has gone from 55-60% to 75% today.

This may now be about to reverse. "Because of global warming we will expand the Cabernets, but it's a slow process," Nicolas de Bailliencourt says. Generally this is more likely to be Cabernet Franc than Cabernet Sauvignon. Although some producers are experimenting with Cabernet Sauvignon, most feel that Cabernet Franc is a better match with the soil and climate. This may be partly due to the fact that the authorities forced them to plan some Cabernet Sauvignon in the 1960s, and as it was mostly not in very suitable places, they haven't had good experiences with it.

Pomerol produces some of the most expensive wines in the world, but the village contains little besides the church, which is surrounded by some of the best vineyards .

Away from the plateau, the soils are sandier, with varying proportions of gravel: here, to the west and south, the wines are lighter and fruity, but rarely rise to those heights of power and complexity characteristic of the châteaux of the plateau. It's often said of Pomerol that you can taste the iron in the soil. This refers to *casse de fer*, deposits of iron, but there is considerable doubt as to whether and what effect this actually has on the wine.

Pomerol's fame is relatively recent: it was scarcely known outside the region until the second half of the twentieth century. The halo effect of top châteaux is more evident in Pomerol than anywhere else; there is little cheap Pomerol. The best wines have an openly sensuous style, which is why Pomerol is sometimes called the Burgundy of Bordeaux. This is completely different from the structure and restraint of the Médoc, even in the present era of increased ripeness everywhere.

Moueix is by far the most important proprietor in Pomerol, and recently has turned away from the negociant business to concentrate on the top châteaux. The range of Moueix châteaux encapsulates the variations in Pomerol. At the very peak is Petrus, now 100% Merlot. Nonetheless it has the structure to age. "The level of tannins is comparable to Château Latour, but the tannins are more approachable, they are Merlot tannins not Cabernet Sauvignon," says Elisabeth Jaubert at Petrus.

Petrus is the most famous property in Pomerol; the buildings used to be shabby but are now quite smart, although still modest in style.

Whereas Petrus is famously on clay, Château Trotanoy is more on gravel, and the wine has a more upright, masculine style. It's still rich and opulent, but the structure can be more overt. La Fleur-Petrus is relatively light for Pomerol, with a fresher impression than Petrus or Trotanoy. And then the most recent creation, Hosanna (carved out of the breakup of Château Certan-Giraud) is unusual for Moueix, with 30% Cabernet Franc giving the tightest, most elegant style. Yet there is a common thread: that initial impression of opulence.

There are a few garage wines in Pomerol, with Le Pin the most often cited, but actually it's really just a very small vineyard with good terroir. Jacques Thienpont, who acquired Le Pin in 1979, admits Le Pin may have been confused with (and have become a model for) the garage wines, but says, "We knew this was special terroir, wine was always made at the cellar here. It's 100% Merlot, but I don't have the power and richness of Petrus, Le Pin is more elegant."

Given the small size of its vineyards, Pomerol really doesn't have much need of garage wines. The issue with Pomerol is not so much the quality of the top wines, which can scarcely be bettered if you like the very lush, opulent style of fully ripe Merlot-dominated cuvées, but the lower quality of wines that come from the lighter, sandy soils. Without any classification, price is really the only guide.

Aside from an unofficial classification in a guide to wines of France in 1943, there has never been any formal ranking of the châteaux. The leading châteaux have no need of one, and the other châteaux have more to lose than to gain. However, it's interesting to list the wines according to recent prices. It is no surprise that Petrus comes at the top, followed by Le Pin and Lafleur.

The interesting thing about these properties is that they are all completely different: Petrus is full-force opulence, Le Pin has as much sense of precision as power, and Lafleur's atypical composition for Pomerol of equal parts of Merlot and Cabernet Franc gives more overt structure. The exact order and grouping of the wines that follow would certainly be open to discussion, but it is beyond debate that they define the heart of Pomerol, all from vineyards located on the plateau.

The balance between the left bank and the right bank has shifted since 1982. For about a century, the 1855 classification was very much the public face of Bordeaux, placing the emphasis almost exclusively on the Médoc. But today's list of the top hundred wines in Bordeaux (judged by price) is split between left and right banks. Pomerol and St. Emilion have been better poised to satisfy the modern craving for rich, intense, ripe if not over-ripe, wines. The rise of the right bank is shown by the way its wines dominate the top fifty.

A Pomerol Classification
Petrus
Le Pin
Château Lafleur
Château La Fleur-Petrus
Château L'Église Clinet
Château Trotanoy
Château L'Évangile
Vieux Château Certan
Château Hosanna
Château La Conseillante
Chateau Bon Pasteur
Clos l'Église
Château Clinet
Château Le Gay
La Fleur de Gay
Château Gazin
Chateau Lafleur Gazin
Château Latour à Pomerol
Château Nénin
Château Petit Village

The leading châteaux of Pomerol are ordered into three groups.

20

1-10

Petrus
Le Pin
Château Ausone
Château Lafite Rothschild
Château Latour
Château Lafleur
Château Cheval Blanc
Château Margaux
Château Mouton Rothschild
Château Haut Brion

11-20

Château Angélus
Château Pavie
La Mondotte
Carruades de Lafite
Château La Mission Haut Brion
Chapelle D'Ausone
Les Forts de Latour
Château de Valandraud
Château Palmer
Château Lafleur Petrus

21-30

Château L'Église Clinet
Château Bellevue Mondotte
Château Léoville Lascases
Le Petit Mouton
Château Trotanoy
Château Le Tertre Rôteboeuf
Petit Cheval
Vieux Château Certan
Château l'Évangile
Château Ducru Beaucaillou
Château Cos d'Estournel

30-40

Gracia
Hosanna
Pavillon Rouge du Château Margaux
Château Pavie-Decesse
Château Pichon Lalande
Château Lynch Bages
Château La Conseillante
Château Magrez Fombrauge
Château Pichon Baron

41-50

Château Montrose
Château Pape Clément
Château Figeac
Château Pontet-Canet
Le Dôme
Château Clinet
Clos Fourtet
Château Beychevelle
Château Le Gay
Château Léoville-Poyferré

51-60

Château Péby-Faugères
Château Duhart Milon Rothschild
Château Troplong Mondot
Château la Fleur de Gay
Château Lascombes
Château Smith Haut Lafitte
Château Pavie Macquin
Clos l'Église
Château Léoville-Barton
Château Calon Ségur

61-70

Château Canon La Gaffelière
Château Canon
Château Haut Bailly
Château Gazin
Château Rauzan-Ségla
Château Clerc Milon
Château Certan de May
Alter Ego de Palmer
Château Trottevieille
Château d'Issan

71-80

Château Malescot-Saint-Exupéry
Château Latour à Pomerol
Château Beausejour Duffau
Château Clos de Sarpe
Château La Gaffelière
Château Petit Village
Château Gruaud Larose
Château Bon Pasteur
Château Branaire Ducru
Château Boyd Cantenac

81-90

Le Carillon de L'Angélus
Château Grand Puy Lacoste
Domaine de Chevalier
Château Monbousquet
Château La Lagune
Château Saint Pierre
Château Talbot
Château Cantenac Brown
Château Lafleur-Gazin
Château Beauséjour-Bécot

91-100

Château Larcis Ducasse
Château Giscours
Château Kirwan
Château Roc de Cambes
Château d'Armailhac
Château Durfort Vivens
Château les Carmes-Haut-Brion
Château Lagrange
Clos du Marquis
Château Marquis de Terme

The top 100 red wines of Bordeaux classified by price include equal numbers from the right bank (gray) and the left bank (black). There are 8 second wines and 6 garage wines.

Satellites and Côtes de Bordeaux

Going north from St. Emilion and Pomerol across the Barbanne stream, you come to the various satellite appellations. Here the soils are clay-limestone, similar to St. Emilion itself (and distinctly better than the soils on the plain of St. Emilion to the south). The result is an inconsistency: although there are few wines in the satellites that really reach the heights, many are at least as good as the so-called Grand Cru St. Emilions coming from the plain.

The St. Emilion satellites (parts of which used to be included in St. Emilion itself) are slightly cooler than St. Emilion, as a result of greater distance from the Dordogne. They are not very well distinguished from one another.

Lalande de Pomerol has more varied soils, with quite a bit of gravel, changing from clay in the east to sand in the west. The wines here are solid rather than refined.

There is no useful distinction to be made between Fronsac and the smaller area of Canon-Fronsac embedded within it (supposedly of higher quality). The wines of Fronsac were well regarded in the eighteenth century, but today are not at all well known. The style is Merlot-based, but less refined than Pomerol.

Côtes de Bordeaux is a new, and not completely coherent, concept. As elsewhere in France, "Côtes" indicates an area that rises above the generic AOP, but without really establishing its own distinctive character. In the case of Bordeaux, there used to be five separate Côtes: Bourg, Blaye, Cadillac, Castillon, and Francs. This was a significant part of the confusion created by the excessive number of AOCs in Bordeaux, so it was decided to merge them into a single Côtes. As Côtes de Bourg did not agree, it remained independent, but the other four are now known as the Côtes de Bordeaux, although each individual area may append its own name.

The Côtes are relatively important in terms of quantity, accounting for about 14% of Bordeaux's production, but the individual areas are quite separate. Bourg and Blaye are well to the north, Francs and Castillon are well to the east of Libourne, and Cadillac is a tiny area adjacent to the Garonne better known for sweet wine.

At the northern extremity of the right bank, Blaye and Bourg are relatively cool climates. Vineyards run up to the Gironde. Yet there is a surprising amount of Cabernet Sauvignon, and this area is the last holdout for Malbec in Bordeaux. There's also a little white wine la-

Reference Wines for the Right Bank	
St. Emilion	Canon La Gaffelière
Pomerol	L'Évangile
Lalande de Pomerol	La Fleur de Boüard
St Georges - St. Emilion	Moulin St. Georges
Côtes de Bourg	Fougas Maldoror
Fronsac	Château Fontenil
Côtes de Castillon	Château d'Aiguilhe

beled as Premières Côtes de Blaye. The best wines come from Bourg, notably from Châteaux Roc de Cambes (clearly *hors de classe*) and Fougas Maldoror, but these are strong exceptions.

Immediately to the east of St. Emilion, Côtes de Castillon produces only red wine from the usual right bank blend. Some producers from St. Emilion have established outposts here, looking for vineyards with good terroir at more reasonable prices. Oenologist Stéphane Derenoncourt (at Domaine de l'A), and Stephan von Neipperg from Canon La Gaffelière (at Château d'Aiguilhe) are the top examples. The best wines are equivalent to St. Emilion.

"Castillon is an extension of the limestone plateau of St. Emilion, and it's a bit cooler here. The difference between the appellations for me is the price. In St. Emilion you have a market price that lets you make sacrifices with lower yields. Castillon can make wines that will compete with St. Emilion (although not with the top Grand Cru Classés). We can make a wine here that reflects its terroir, much better than the plain of St. Emilion. The aging potential is similar to St. Emilion," says Stéphane Derenoncourt. But Castillon's obscurity is an impediment. "The problem is economic. Even in France, Castillon is totally unknown. More than half the wines of Castillon are declassified to Bordeaux because it is easier for the negociants to sell. We are victims of the appellation."

"Entre-deux-Mers does not have a specific terroir: its characteristics come from assemblage from diverse terroirs, often varying from one parcel to the next," says the producers' organization. This is a major source for white wine just one notch above the generic Bordeaux AOP; but the reds are labeled as Bordeaux AOP. Following the translation of the name as "between two seas," "between" is a good description for the wines. There is little that really stands out here. Cooperatives are unusually important, given the economic difficulties of lesser regions of Bordeaux.

Visiting the Region

The town of St. Emilion is the tourist center, with hotels, restaurants, and a huge number of wine shops. Until recently it was really the only game around, but now some châteaux have opened restaurants, and even offer accommodation, so there are more choices to the both the west and east of St. Emilion. Close to Cheval Blanc, the restaurant Terrasse Rouge is on the roof of the futuristic cuverie at Château La Dominique, with sunset views from Cheval Blanc to the church at Pomerol. To the east of the village, there is now a restaurant at Château Troplong Mondot.

The town offers easy access to the châteaux of St. Emilion and Pomerol. It's somewhat easier to find your way around to the west; to the east, the terrain is hillier and it's easy to get lost in the little roads. Châteaux are not always well signposted, so allow plenty of time to find producers.

Bordeaux is much less tourist-oriented than other wine regions, such as Burgundy. It is only in the last decade or so, after all, that châteaux have been receptive to visits. It's a major sign of the change in attitude that, whereas in the past châteaux would never sell directly to consumers, now most except the grandest will do so. Today most châteaux will receive visitors, although usually an appointment is required; it is relatively rare to find a dedicated tasting room that is open to tourists.

Visits tend to be relatively short. A typical routine is to start by walking to the edge of vineyards, then making a tour of the winemaking facilities, and finishing up with a brief tasting, likely to encompass the current vintage of both the grand vin and the second wine (if any). It is rare that a château produces more than two wines, and it's not common to be offered more than one vintage. You rarely get barrel samples in Bordeaux. Allowing an hour for a visit is sufficient in planning a schedule.

Whether because the châteaux regard themselves as too grand to need a street address, or because each town is really quite small, the address is often nothing more than a zip code and a town name. This does not necessarily mean the château will be right in the center, however, so allow extra time to find it, because your GPS is unlikely to be able to find the château by name. This is especially true for the area to the east of St. Emilion, where it's easy to take a wrong turn in the rabbit warren of roads.

The etiquette of tasting assumes you will spit. A producer will be surprised if you drink the wine. Usually a tasting room or cellar is equipped with spittoons, but ask if you do not see one (crachoir in French). Of course, some tourists do enjoy drinking the wines, but producers will take you more seriously if you spit.

Vintages

Since the trend to warmer vintages started in 1982, there has been a zigzag between years producing increasingly riper conditions and reversion to the old "classic" conditions. The vintages of 1990 and 2000 might be considered directly in the line of 1982; 2005 was richer yet, and then 2009 was the richest vintage of all; 2010 is in the same line, but more structured without really be-coming classic. (This is to ignore real heatwaves, such as the "canicule" of 2003, which went far beyond the bounds). Lesser years are much better than they used to be: whereas 1984 and 1987, and then 1991 and 1997 were all but write-offs, 2007, 2008, and 2011 are decent.

		The Twenty-First Century
2017	*	A difficult vintage with rather small production, but quality is generally good. Some châteaux may not produce grand vin because of heavy losses due to frost early in the season.
2016	***	Wet for the first half of the season, dry for the second half, but shaping up to be an excellent vintage, the best since 2010.
2015	**	An attractive vintage, more restrained than usual on the right bank, with very nice wines for the mid term. St. Emilion tends to elegance, Pomerol is more structured than usual.
2014	*	Not a great vintage, but better than the preceding three years. A cool summer was followed by the longest Indian summer on record, with perfect sunny conditions into October. High acidity, good tannins, high but not excessive alcohol, gave elegance rather than power.
2013		Cool Spring made for a very slow start to season with uneven flowering, leading to late harvest at the start of

		October. Acidity is high, fruits are light and more often in the red spectrum; these are wines to enjoy young before the fruits fade. Just over half the usual size, this was the smallest harvest since 1991.
2012	*	"Lovely restaurant wine" is the phrase that appears most often in my tasting notes of this vintage. It's generally described as a Merlot year. St. Emilion is relatively soft, but Pomerol is more structured than usual.
2011		Saved from disaster by fine conditions in September, but uneven. On the right bank, St. Emilion tends to cover up the problems with an edge of apparent sweetness, but the wines won't last; Pomerol is more even, but superficial. Not a very generous vintage, drink before it goes flat.
2010	***	The vintage is as ripe as 2009, but acidity and tannins are higher, giving a more classic impression. The conventional description is that this is more classic and will be longer lived, but I am not so certain the fruits will outlive the tannins and acidity into really old age. On both left and right banks the wines tend to elegance rather than power.
2009	***	Reputed to be so rich as to break tradition, but in fact showing surprising freshness on release. Ripe, round, and attractive already: very possibly longer lived than general commentary would suggest, but probably not destined to be a very old vintage in classic tradition.
2008		Rain at the beginning and end of the season was the problem this year. There's variation from dilute impressions to more classic wines, but these are wines for the short term.
2007		Wines are lighter, due to cool and wet conditions, and for short term consumption.
2006	*	The wines tend to be a little flat, with not quite enough fruit, resulting from alternating hot and cold periods during the growing season. Wines of the right bank lack their usual richness.
2005	***	A great year with perfect conditions following the precedent of 1982. Certainly a vintage in the modern idiom, but without the excesses that were to come in 2009 and 2010. The wines should mature to elegance and finesse.

2004	**	A classic restaurant vintage: well balanced wines for mid term drinking, now at, or sometimes passing, their peak.
2003	*	The year of the canicule. Don't believe the propaganda that acidity suddenly corrected itself and the wines came into balance: they tend to be clumsy and over-extracted; even the first growths did not escape.
2002		The vintage is usually described as classic, but does not really have the concentration to pull off the style.
2001	*	A nice well balanced vintage at the outset, perhaps similar to 2004 in style, but with a bit less concentration, and higher acidity and more evident tannins, so now moving past its peak.
	Bordeaux Vintages 2000-1991	
2000	***	Another in the series of vintages following the model of 1982, but with some of the wines surprisingly tiring at this point. The best may mature in a classic direction.
1999	*	Lighter wines, with the best superficially attractive, but nothing pro-found. On balance probably just a bit better than 1998, although this may vary.
1998	**	One of those vintages with a distinct difference between left and right banks. The right bank is very good, whereas the left bank suffered from rain.
1997		A large crop with problems of dilution and lack of ripeness; not of interest today.
1996	*	Never as good on the right bank as on the left bank, but in both cases, as the wines mature, herbaceousness is over-taking the fruits, making this a distinct throwback.
1995	**	Another generally dry year with good concentration, fine on both left and right banks; in the modern idiom, but still going strong.
1994		Overrated (because of the previous three years); wines were rich and agreeable at first, but in any case are not now of interest.

1993		An improvement from the previous years but no longer of interest.
1992		A poor vintage now of little interest, with wines diluted by rainfall.
1991		The first (and worst) of four uninteresting years.
	Bordeaux Vintages 1990-1982	
1990	***	The better of a pair of back to back promising vintages. An excellent growing season and good harvest conditions led to well balanced wines. On paper, very similar to 1989, but the wines today show an undeniable increase in finesse over 1989, perhaps because harvest was later in 1990.
1989	**	Initially this seemed along the lines of 1982, with warm conditions giving ripe wines. The best wines have developed in a delicious direction, but too many seem powerful rather than elegant, sometimes giving a touch of rusticity. Pomerol is better than St. Emilion.
1988	*	More inclined to power than elegance, slow to come around, with the best wines having classic structure, although others may seem a little clumsy.
1987		A poor vintage now of little interest.
1986	**	Often described as a classic vintage, meaning good tannic structure, so not as good on the right bank as on the left bank.
1985	**	A delicious, forward vintage, often described as charming, and equally good on left and right banks.
1984		A poor vintage now of little interest.
1983	**	A very good vintage, although not up to 1982. More consistent on the right bank than the left bank.
1982	***	The great vintage that started the modern era. Initially fruit-forward and accessible, then closing up in the late nineties, and from year 2000 reverting to type with a touch of herbaceous often balancing the fruits. The best wines are still splendid and classic.

Maps

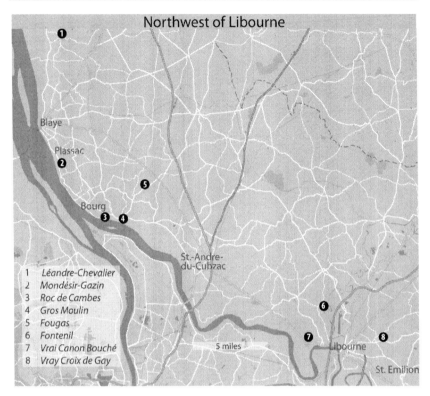

Northwest of Libourne

Blaye

Plassac

Bourg

St.-Andre-
du-Cubzac

Libourne

St. Emilion

5 miles

1   Léandre-Chevalier
2   Mondésir-Gazin
3   Roc de Cambes
4   Gros Moulin
5   Fougas
6   Fontenil
7   Vrai Canon Bouché
8   Vray Croix de Gay

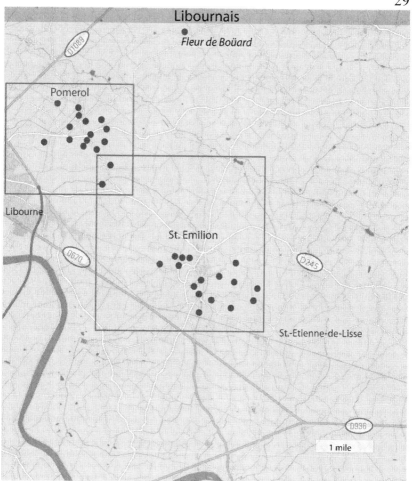

30

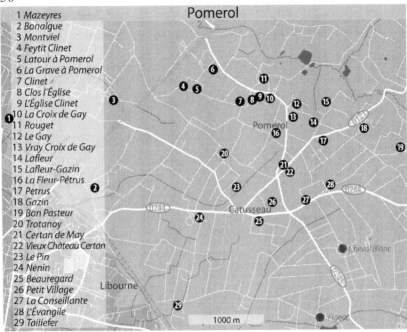

Pomerol

1 Mazeyres
2 Bonalgue
3 Montviel
4 Feytit Clinet
5 Latour à Pomerol
6 La Grave à Pomerol
7 Clinet
8 Clos l'Église
9 L'Église Clinet
10 La Croix de Gay
11 Rouget
12 Le Gay
13 Vray Croix de Gay
14 Lafleur
15 Lafleur-Gazin
16 La Fleur-Pétrus
17 Petrus
18 Gazin
19 Bon Pasteur
20 Trotanoy
21 Certan de May
22 Vieux Château Certan
23 Le Pin
24 Nénin
25 Beauregard
26 Petit Village
27 La Conseillante
28 L'Évangile
29 Taillefer

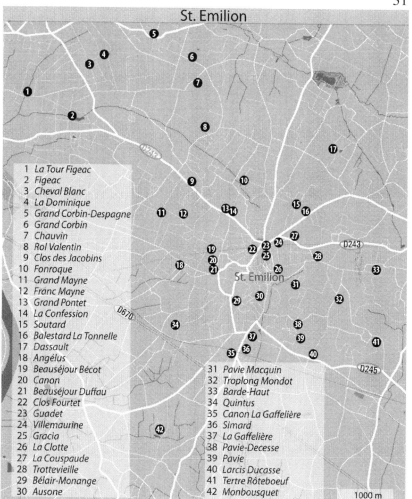

St. Emilion

1 La Tour Figeac
2 Figeac
3 Cheval Blanc
4 La Dominique
5 Grand Corbin-Despagne
6 Grand Corbin
7 Chauvin
8 Rol Valentin
9 Clos des Jacobins
10 Fonroque
11 Grand Mayne
12 Franc Mayne
13 Grand Pontet
14 La Confession
15 Soutard
16 Balestard La Tonnelle
17 Dassault
18 Angélus
19 Beauséjour Bécot
20 Canon
21 Beauséjour Duffau
22 Clos Fourtet
23 Guadet
24 Villemaurine
25 Gracia
26 La Clotte
27 La Couspaude
28 Trottevieille
29 Bélair-Monange
30 Ausone
31 Pavie Macquin
32 Troplong Mondot
33 Barde-Haut
34 Quintus
35 Canon La Gaffelière
36 Simard
37 La Gaffelière
38 Pavie-Decesse
39 Pavie
40 Larcis Ducasse
41 Tertre Rôteboeuf
42 Monbousquet

1000 m

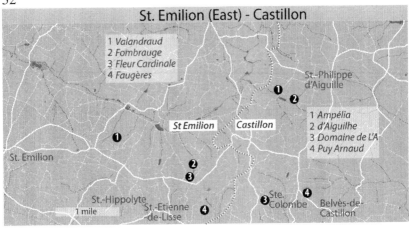

Profiles of Leading Châteaux

Ratings	
****	Sui generis, standing out above everything else in the appellation
***	Excellent producers defining the very best of the appellation
**	Top producers whose wines typify the appellation
*	Very good producers making wines of character that rarely disappoint

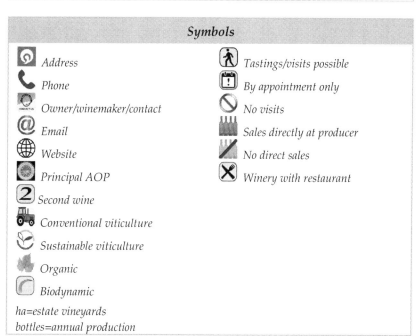

Symbols

Address	Tastings/visits possible
Phone	By appointment only
Owner/winemaker/contact	No visits
Email	Sales directly at producer
Website	No direct sales
Principal AOP	Winery with restaurant
Second wine	
Conventional viticulture	
Sustainable viticulture	
Organic	
Biodynamic	

ha=estate vineyards
bottles=annual production

Domaine de L'A   *

11 Lieu-dit Fillol,33350 Sainte-Colombe

(33) 005 57 24 60 29

Christine & Stéphane Derenoncourt

contact@domainedela.com

www.domainedela.com

Côtes de Castillon

12 ha; 45,000 bottles
[map p. 32]

Stéphane Derenoncourt is known worldwide as a consulting oenologist. He is especially prominent on Bordeaux's right bank, where he established Domaine de l'A in the satellite area of Castillon in 1999. Loans from local vignerons enabled him to buy a couple of hectares of south-facing calcareous terroir on a high point, and he built the first cuverie with the help of some friends. Planting density was increased by interspersing additional rows between the existing rows of vines, the vineyard was later expanded by buying two more plots, and the mix was brought to 80% Merlot and 20% Cabernet Franc.

Stéphane believes that Castillon has the potential to rival St. Emilion, and sets out to prove it with his domain. Together with Château d'Aiguilhe (for which he consults), it's become one of the defining properties for the appellation. What typicity do you want in Domaine de l'A, I asked? "Expression calcaire. I love calcaire, it's the rock that gives the best transformation for red wine," Stéphane says. "On calcareous soil, Merlot is fresh and gives flowers and minerality or salinity."

The first vintage was 2000. The style is well structured, perhaps a little sturdy. It can be a little lacking in generosity in difficult years. It needs time, beginning to develop after five or six years, with minerality showing as a touch of gunflint. When young, fruits are dense and quite extracted. The 65% new oak can be quite evident.

Château d'Aiguilhe

*

CHATEAU D'AIGUILHE

2005

CÔTES DE CASTILLON

APPELLATION CÔTES DE CASTILLON CONTRÔLÉE

S.C.E.A. DU CHATEAU D'AIGUILHE
PROPRIÉTAIRE RÉCOLTANT - ST PHILIPPE D'AIGUILHE - GIRONDE - FRANCE
www.neipperg.com

MIS EN BOUTEILLE AU CHATEAU

13,5% vol.   PRODUCE OF FRANCE - VIN DE BORDEAUX
CONTIENT DES SULFATES - CONTAINS SULPHITES   75 cl

63 Bourg-est, 33350 Saint Philippe d'Aiguille

(33) 05 57 40 60 10

Stephan von Neipperg

info@neipperg.com

www.neipperg.com

Côtes de Castillon

Seigneurs d'Aiguilhe

70 ha; 220,000 bottles

[map p. 32]

Stephan von Neipperg of Château Canon La Gaffelière in St. Emilion was ahead of his time when he purchased Château d'Aiguilhe in 1998. It's an old estate that at one point had 400 ha of vines. The name, which means needle or peak, reflects its location on a rocky outcrop, just across the boundary with St. Emilion.

The place was run down when Stephan purchased it. "When I took over we preserved 27 ha of old vines, we took out 16 ha of poor Cabernet Franc and Sauvignon," he says. The planting mix is now 80% Merlot and 20% Cabernet Franc; there is no Cabernet Sauvignon because, "We are on chalk, and chalk and Cabernet Sauvignon is a disaster." The average vine age of 30 years reflects a large gap between the preserved old vines and the new plantings.

The estate extends over 110 ha and includes a ruined fourteenth century fortress. Old buildings have been restored and a new cuverie constructed. Stéphane Derenoncourt, of Domaine de l'A, is the consulting oenologist. Coming mostly from young vines, the second wine is about a third of production. The grand vin has a nicely structured impression coming from the Cabernet Franc (and 50% new oak). There can be quite a mineral impression when young, and it develops quite slowly, reaching a peak after about ten years, but staying fresh and lively. It's an interesting contrast with Clos de l'Oratoire, a grand cru St. Emilion in the Neipperg portfolio, which is lighter and rounder, but without Aiguilhe's mineral depth.

Château Angélus ***

33330 St. Emilion

(33) 05 57247139

angelus@angelus.com

www.angelus.com

St. Emilion

Carillon d'Angélus

42 ha; 140,000 bottles
[map p. 31]

From the magnificent set of bells (programmed to play your national anthem on arrival) to the vast entrance hall with a vaulted wooden roof set to rival the largest in Europe, it is evident that no expense was spared in constructing the new château. It's so massive and convoluted that you are left wondering where to find the working winery. Before there was just a cuverie, but Hubert de Boüard wanted to build a Château.

The Boüard's have owned Angélus since 1782. The vineyards are in a large single holding, facing south on a gentle slope. Angélus uses 27 ha; Carillon comes from 12 ha that are not classified. The vineyard was expanded in the sixties and seventies, but the proportions of 50% Merlot, 47% Cabernet Franc, and 3% Cabernet Sauvignon have not changed since Hubert's grandfather planted the vineyards, focusing on Cabernet Franc to produce more structured wine. The large amount of Cabernet Franc is "just like it is at Cheval Blanc and Ausone."

Hubert changed the style after he came to Angélus in 1979, reducing yields and improving quality. All this was rewarded with promotion to Premier Grand Cru Classé A in 2012 (and commemorated by an engraving in stone at the entrance to the new building). Merlot is vinified in stainless steel to preserve fruit, but Cabernet Franc in concrete, malolactic occurs in barrique, and Angélus matures in 100% new oak for up to two years. The wine has all the refinement of ripe Cabernet. In addition to the second wine, there is a third wine, N 3 d'Angélus.

Château Ausone

****

⌖ *Ausone, 33330 St. Emilion*

📞 *(33) 05 57 24 68 88*

👤 *Alain Vauthier*

@ *chateau.ausone@wanadoo.fr*

🌐 *chateau-ausone.fr*

◉ *St. Emilion*

② *Chapelle D'Ausone*

🚫

◖ *8 ha; 24,000 bottles*
[map p. 31]

Ausone is a small property, with a very discrete access track just besides the town of St. Emilion. About a quarter of its vineyards are immediately around; the rest are on the surrounding slopes. Now clearly one of the top wines of St. Emilion, every drop a first growth, Château Ausone had a chequered history for the last quarter of the twentieth century. A family dispute led to arguments about who was in charge, with constant disagreements about routine issues such as date of harvest, but this was resolved when (following a legal action) Alain Vauthier took over the estate in 1995. Since then the wine has gone from strength to strength.

The unusually high proportion of Cabernet Franc, which is just over half of plantings, is the driving force for Ausone's style. "In the top terroirs I have more Cabernet Franc than Merlot," Alain says. "It's the Cabernet Franc that makes Ausone," says Maitre de Chai Philippe Baillarguet. There's an ongoing experiment with Cabernet Sauvignon; enough has been planted to make four barriques. At the moment it goes into the second wine, "but it's almost sure some will go into the grand vin when the vines are older," Philippe says. The style shows purity of fruits, balance rather than excess, structure for aging, and that indefinable quality: breed. The mark of Ausone is constant questioning in viticulture and vinification as to what will make the best wine. The Vauthier family also owns two other châteaux in St. Emilion, Moulin St. Georges and Fonbel.

38

Château Beauregard *

73 Rue de Catusseau, 33500 Pomerol

(33) 05 57 51 13 36

Vincent Priou

contact@chateau-beauregard.com

www.chateau-beauregard.com

Pomerol

Le Benjamin de Beauregard

18 ha; 160,000 bottles   [map p. 30]

One of the largest estates in Pomerol, this property was sold in 2014 by the bank Crédit Foncière that had owned it since 1991 to a syndicate of the Moulins of Galeries Lafayette and the Cathiards of Château Smith Haut Lafitte. The sale also included Château Pavillon Beauregard in Lalande de Pomerol (the wine is made at Beauregard), and Château Bastor-Lamontagne in Sauternes. Based on a soil map, vineyards are being planted on a 12-year program, and the old cellars have been replaced with a new gravity-feed winery, completed in 2015 in a style that matches the gracious old château.

At the southeast of the Pomerol plateau, close to St. Emilion, the major part of the vineyard surrounds the château and is planted with 70% Merlot and 30% Cabernet Franc. It is sandier at the south and more gravelly in the north. The second wine comes mostly from younger vines, and has increased from 40% to 50% of production; it may increase to 60% as the planting program progresses. The second wine also includes some specific parcels, such as Cabernet Franc from sandier soils, and usually has a little more Merlot.

The old stainless steel tanks have been replaced with concrete tanks with heating/cooling coils embedded in the walls. There's all the latest equipment including an optical sorter. The wine has malolactic fermentation in barriques, and then the grand vin stays for 18 months (with 60% new oak), and the second wine has 12 months in 20% new oak, before it is blended.

The château has been regarded as a modernist since the style was lightened in 1998. With its high content of Cabernet Franc—"The high use of Cabernet Franc to give freshness is really the nature of Beauregard," they say at the château—the wine does not have the super-opulence of some Pomerols; it's more like St. Emilion. It has tended to give a somewhat superficial impression: the 2009 lacks stuffing, the taut character of 2010 shows success for the vintage, 2011 seems superficial, 2012 shows more structure, 2014 moves towards a light elegance, 2015 shows more depth. The new regime is increasing precision, the main evident change being increased refinement in the tannins, to give a greater sense of sophistication. The second wine is pleasant but does not have the character of the grand vin.

Château Beauséjour Bécot ★★

Beauséjour, 33330 St. Emilion

(33) 05 57 74 46 87

Julien Barthe & Juliette Bécot

contact@beausejour-becot.com

www.beausejour-becot.com

St. Emilion

Petit Bécot

22 ha; 80,000 bottles
[map p. 31]

"This estate has belonged to my family since the French Revolution," says Juliette Bécot. Her grandfather owned a 5 ha property called Château La Carte, which he worked at weekends. At the end of the sixties, he purchased Beauséjour, which together with La Carte was 12 ha, and renamed Beauséjour Bécot. (The original estate was named Beauséjour in 1787, and was divided in 1869. The other half today is called Beauséjour Duffau-Lagarosse.) Juliette's father, Gérard, retired in 2014. Juliette is the winemaker, and her husband, Julien Barthe, is the general manager.

There have been complications with purchases of other vineyards. Gérard bought Trois Moulins, the highest point in St. Emilion, in the seventies; he thought it was the highest quality terroir, but Beauséjour was demoted in 1986 because of its inclusion; it regained its status as a Premier Grand Cru Classé in 1996. "It was hard during this period because the consumer doesn't understand why you lost your classification. The positive side was that we had to make a lot of effort, we introduced green harvest and sorting earlier than other châteaux," Juliette now says.

Located on the limestone plateau just outside the town, Beauséjour's vineyards have 70% Merlot, but are changing. In 1995, Gérard bought the 2.4 ha vineyard of La Gomerie. As it was not possible to include it in Beauséjour Bécot, it was vinified separately, acquiring a reputation as a garage wine. Since 2012 it has been part of Beauséjour Bécot. "It has 100% Merlot, and after the last classification we were allowed to include it in Beauséjour Bécot, so we have more Merlot," Juliette explains. Effectively the varietal composition has changed from an average of 70% Merlot until 2011, to an average of 80% since 2012. The Merlot is typically very ripe, and this shows by making Beauséjour a little smoother, but it remains elegantly restrained. "Beauséjour Bécot brings the structure, La Gomerie the fat," is how Juliette describes it. Juliette also bought an estate in Castillon in 2001, where she makes wine under the label of Joanin Bécot.

Château Beauséjour Héritiers Duffau Lagar- **
rosse

Premier Grand Cru Classé

CHÂTEAU BEAUSÉJOUR

Saint-Emilion Grand Cru
APPELLATION SAINT-EMILION GRANDCRU CONTRÔLÉE

S.C. Château Beauséjour
Héritiers Duffau Lagarosse
Propriétaires à Saint-Emilion (Gironde) France
MIS EN BOUTEILLE AU CHÂTEAU

Beauséjour, 33330 St. Emilion

(33) 05 57 24 71 61

Nicolas Thienpont

beausejourhdl@beausejourhdl.com

www.beausejourhdl.com

St. Emilion

Croix de Beauséjour

7 ha; 25,000 bottles
[map p. 31]

One of the smallest Premier Grand Cru Classés, this has been owned by the same family since 1847 and is now in the hands of the seventh generation, but is managed by Nicolas Thienpont. The estate has not changed since it was created in 1869 by dividing the 14.5 ha of the original Beauséjour. This part has the original house, and under the château are extensive limestone caves from the Roman era. The estate lies in an amphitheater protected from the north wind, with a plateau falling off to the south and southwest.

Plantings are one third Cabernet Franc and two thirds Merlot. Five zones in the vineyards are vinified separately. Vinification is in concrete vats. Grapes are destemmed but not crushed, indigenous yeast start fermentation in three days, and it lasts 10-12 days. Both pump-over and punch-down are used depending on the lot. "It's not the usual approach in Bordeaux but it suits us very well," says winemaker David Suire. The small vat room looks a bit old fashioned, very WYSIWG, with no glitzy renovation here.

Lots go into new or old wood depending on character, and MLF occurs in barriques. There is 60-65% new oak for the grand vin and no new oak for the second wine. "For us the most important determinant between grand vin and second wine is the terroir," David says. The first racking after malo is the main point of selection. The style is mainstream for St. Emilion, which is to say focused on the ripeness of Merlot, but can be a little sturdy.

Château Bélair-Monange

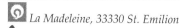

La Madeleine, 33330 St. Emilion

(33) 05 57 51 78 96

Geneviève Sandifer

info@jpmoueix.com

www.moueix.com

St. Emilion

Annonce

24 ha; 30,000 bottles

[map p. 31]

With vineyards divided between the limestone plateau and the slopes near Château Ausone, this should be one of the top châteaux of St. Emilion. As Château Belair, however, it was never very successful, perhaps due to the idiosyncrasies of its former owner. Purchased by Moueix in 2008, the name was changed to Bélair-Monange in memory of Christian Moueix's grandmother, and an enormous program of investment began, with vineyards extensively replanted, and the château rebuilt.

Yet there was scarcely a chance to see the effects before Moueix announced that Bélair-Monange was to be merged with Château Magdelaine close by. Owned by Moueix since 1952, Magdelaine has been impeccably run, and has been one of my favorite St. Emilions. Although its proportion of Merlot was the highest in St. Emilion at 90%, the wine has always been refined and elegant. Perhaps for that reason, it was never completely successful in the marketplace.

The fig leaf for the merger is that the complementary character of the two properties will allow a better wine to be made than either alone. "We have big ambitions for Bélair-Monange," says Frédéric Lospied at Moueix. Certainly the combined property will have vineyards as impressive as any in St. Emilion. From 2012, the wine from the combined properties is labeled as Bélair-Monange; whether it will follow Magdelaine's discrete style remains to be seen. In the meantime, Magdelaine 2009 and 2010 are still available.

Château Bon Pasteur ★★

10, Chemin de Maillet, 33500 Pomerol

(33) 05 57 51 52 43

Benoit Prevot

contact@chateaulebonpasteur.com

www.chateaulebonpasteur.com

Pomerol

l'Etoile de Bon Pasteur

7 ha; 25,000 bottles
[map p. 30]

It might be fair to say that this is the archetypal Rolland wine, since this is Michel Rolland's old family property, where he perfected his style: harvesting very ripe from low yields, performing malolactic fermentation in barriques, and aging in lots of new oak. Located on the border between Pomerol and St. Emilion, vineyards are 80% Merlot and 20% Cabernet Franc, spread over 21 plots, mostly on the plateau of Pomerol. Bon Pasteur and the other Rolland family properties—Chateaux Bertineau St.-Vincent in Lalande de Pomerol, and Rolland Maillet in St. Emilion (close to Bon Pasteur where all the wines are made)—were sold in 2013 to Pan Sutong, of the Goldin investment group in Hong Kong, but Michel continues to advise. A second wine from young vines has been introduced—it's usually 20-30% of production—and there's a program for restructuring the vineyards and investing in the cellars.

A fermentation cellar with stainless steel vats was constructed in 1987. "It was very avant-garde at the time," says Benoit Prevot, who has made the wine at the Rolland family properties for the past 25 years. "M. Rolland is an avant-gardiste." But now half the wine is vinified directly in barriques, using a system that Michel invented in 2000; it was put into full production in 2008. The barrels spin on wheels instead of using pumping-over or punch down for maceration. "Fermentation integrale integrates the wood better, there is no woody character to the wine. This gives tannins that are creamy and supple."

The style by no means shows the overwhelming richness you might expect from the public caricatures of Michel Rolland's style. The 2010 is surprisingly stern, 2011 is typically ripe and soft, 2012 is smooth and taut, 2014 makes a classy impression of elegance albeit rich, and 2015 is nutty, full bodied, and quite structured. The second wine follows house style in showing that coating of richness on top of the character of the vintage. "I would begin to drink the second wine after 5-10 years, and Bon Pasteur after that," Benoit says.

Château Canon

***

Saint Martin, Route Du Milieu, 33330 St. Emilion

(33) 05 57 55 23 45

Nicolas Audebert

contact@chateau-canon.com

www.chateaucanon.com

St. Emilion

Clos Canon

29 ha; 90,000 bottles
[map p. 31]

Overlooking the Church, all around the lieu-dit of Saint Martin at the top of St. Emilion, are gateposts marked Château Canon. Most lead into vineyards or annex buildings; entrance to the château itself was blocked by building works for ages by an extensive restoration. "When we got here there were many problems—which is why no one wanted to buy it—we've been here since 1996 and we only broke even two years ago. Things go very quickly down and it takes a long time to come back. It's taken twenty years to get to where we wanted," says John Kolasa, who took over when the Wertheimer brothers (of Chanel) added Canon to their holding of Rausan-Ségla in Margaux.

The vineyards have been three quarters replanted; the cellars, which were contaminated with TCA, have been completely rebuilt. The 4 ha estate of Curé Bon was incorporated in 2000, and more recently the adjacent 12 ha estate of Matras has been added; in due course it will become the second wine. The most recent purchase, in 2017, was Château Berliquet.

At one point, Canon went up to 80% Merlot while replanting, but now it's back to 65%. "The vines get stressed up here, they get more minerality, the wines will last for years," John says. "I see more Cabernet Franc when I taste Canon than there really is. It's all to do with the terroir, it's the stress on the limestone." Comparing the 2001 and 2011, I see a clear lineage: fine and elegant, never blowsy, more the precision of Cabernet Franc than the roundness of Merlot, a real connoisseur's wine. That sense of elegance and purity runs through all the recent vintages.

Château Canon La Gaffelière ***

📍 33330 St. Emilion

📞 (33) 05 57 24 71 33

Stephan von Neipperg

@ info@neipperg.com

🌐 www.neipperg.com

St. Emilion

2️⃣ Neipperg Selection

🌿 20 ha; 65,000 bottles

[map p. 31]

Comte Stephan de Neipperg, to give him his full title, came from Montpellier in 1983 to take over Canon La Gaffelière, which his father had bought in 1969. At the time, it was a St. Emilion Grand Cru Classé with a middling reputation. In 2012 it was promoted to Premier Grand Cru Classé, and today Vignobles Neipperg owns four châteaux in St. Emilion, and other properties in Castillon and Pessac-Léognan, as well as outside France. The coat of arms is the distinguishing mark on all the brands.

The improvements at Canon La Gaffelière include replanting the vineyards, restricting yields, and renovating the winery, which is a practical building just below the town of St. Emilion. Lying at the base of the Côtes, the south-facing vineyards are 55% Merlot, 40% Cabernet Franc, and a little Cabernet Sauvignon. "Cabernet Franc is difficult in St. Emilion, but if it's good, it makes outstanding wine," Stephan says. "Here we never take the Cabernet Franc out, it's all perpetuated by selection massale. For me it's very important that we are not working with the clones, it's about complexity not volume."

Vinification is in wooden vats, followed by malolactic in barrique, with 80-100% new oak for the grand vin. The wine has gone from strength to strength since the mid nineties, with the high proportion of Cabernet Franc always conveying a sense of finesse; in fact, although Cabernet Franc is the minority grape, I usually feel it is the dominant aromatic influence. That shows in the 2010, more aromatic than usual, the elegance of 2011, faintly savory character of 2012, minerality of 2014, and the supreme elegance and precision of 2015.

Château Certan de May   *

1 Certan, 33500 Pomerol

(33) 05 57 51 41 53

Jean-Luc Barreau

chateau.certan-de-may@wanadoo.fr

Pomerol

6 ha; 24,000 bottles

[map p. 30]

Just across the street from its better known neighbor, Vieux Château Certan, this was once part of the same estate. It became independent when a small parcel was split off and was named Château Certan de May by its owners, the Demay family. It was sold in 1925 to the Barreau-Badard family, who still own it. The estate has been run by Jean-Luc Barreau since 1975, but the wines are marketed exclusively by Moueix. Michel Rolland was the consulting oenologist until 2012; since then it has been Jean-Claude Berrouet.

Consisting of a single parcel on the southeast part of the Pomerol plateau, the terroir has clay and gravel soils. It is planted to 70% Merlot, 25% Cabernet Franc, and 5% Cabernet Sauvignon. This may explain a certain restraint in the wines, as much like St. Emilion as Pomerol.

Fermentation takes place in stainless steel, and is followed by maceration for up to a month. Aging lasts 16 months in up to 70% new barriques. The château seems to have under-performed in vintages from 1989 to 1999, but at least since 2005, has made a very fine impression. The wines are not blockbusters but can be elegant.

Château Cheval Blanc ★★★★

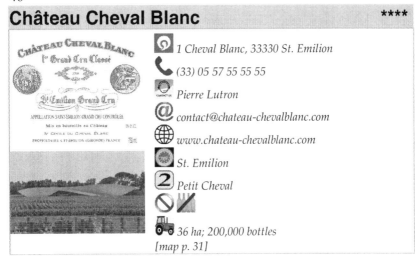

1 Cheval Blanc, 33330 St. Emilion

(33) 05 57 55 55 55

Pierre Lutron

contact@chateau-chevalblanc.com

www.chateau-chevalblanc.com

St. Emilion

Petit Cheval

36 ha; 200,000 bottles
[map p. 31]

Since Cheval Blanc was created by splitting off from Figeac in the 1830s, it's been a defining property in St. Emilion. Yet located adjacent to Pomerol, it is atypical, with mostly gravel soil types. Plantings are 60% Cabernet Franc to 40% Merlot. However, "people who say that Merlot is for clay and Cabernet Franc is for gravel don't understand Cheval Blanc. It's exactly the opposite here," says technical director Pierre Clouet. There's also a small amount of Cabernet Sauvignon: "This is like salt and pepper, we need it."

Cheval Blanc was purchased in 1998 by Bernard Arnault of LVMH, and there has been massive investment in a new, rather controversial winery, completed in 2011. "We respect the nineteenth century patrimony but we are in the twenty-first century and we wanted to build something modern," Pierre explains. The new building has a living roof with a garden, and a cellar equipped with special tanks to handle each of the 45 plots. "We don't want to change the style of Cheval, it was decided two centuries ago. But we want to have more precision, more resolution, more pixels," Pierre says. "The philosophy is that 100% of each plot goes into Cheval or into Petit Cheval. So we produce each plot with the intention of making Cheval, but in any year there may be plots that don't succeed." There is also a third wine.

The compelling richness of the grand vin is offset against a background of finely structured black fruits stopping just short of impressions of tobacco. In 2016, the château launched its first white wine, a 100% Sauvignon Blanc called Le Petit Cheval Blanc.

Château Clinet ★★

2009

CHÂTEAU
C L I N E T
Pomerol

 16 Chemin de Feytit, 33500 Pomerol

 (33) 05 57 25 50 00

 Ronan Laborde

 contact@chateauclinet.com

 www.chateauclinet.com

 Pomerol

 Fleur de Clinet

 12 ha; 45,000 bottles

[map p. 30]

It's been all change at Clinet since the Laborde family purchased the property in 1999. Previously, Clinet was a family property before being sold to an insurance company in 1991. With Michel Rolland as consultant, the style was distinctly full bodied. Ronan Laborde came to run the property after his father purchased it, and in 2004 the building was extended into a very modern winery with huge windows looking out over the vineyard.

At the time of purchase, there were 8.6 ha with 80% Merlot, 15% Cabernet Sauvignon and 5% Cabernet Franc. Ronan changed the balance to more Merlot, and then added some vineyards (close by in Feytit) that are all Merlot, so the plantings are now 90% Merlot. "What we are always looking for here is the creamy touch that is brought by the Merlot, we don't extract too much," Ronan says, explaining that he has backed off from the opulent style of the former ownership. The grand vin sees 60% new oak.

Fleur de Clinet is not strictly a second wine; it has declassified lots from Clinet, but also includes juice and berries purchased from other growers in Pomerol. In addition, there is a Bordeaux AOP simply called Ronan, made in a rented facility while a new winery is being constructed for it. I have found recent vintages of Clinet to be relatively restrained, but in a clean, soft, modern style. "This typifies the style of Clinet I would like to produce," says Ronan about the 2008, which has supple, slightly aromatic, round black fruits. The wine is quite approachable when young.

Château La Confession *

Lieu Dit Haut Pontet, 33330 St. Emilion

(33) 05 57 48 13 13

Jean-Philippe Janoueix

contact@jpjdomaines.com

www.jpjdomaines.com

St. Emilion

Haut-Pontet

8 ha; 45,000 bottles
[map p. 31]

From an old winemaking family on the right bank, Jean-Philippe Janoueix has been expanding his portfolio of châteaux in various right bank appellations since he started his company in 1994. When he purchased La Confession in 2001, it was only 2.5 ha. It has expanded, and plantings today are 70% Merlot. Other properties in his group of boutique wineries are Chateaux La Croix St. Georges and Sacré Coeur in Pomerol, and Cap St. George in St. Georges-St. Emilion. La Confession is one of his stars.

There's a lively spirit of experimentation here. Jean-Philippe is known for pushing the boundaries in planting very dense vineyards; his cuvée 20 Mille comes from a 1.3 ha plot in Fronsac that is planted at 20,000 vines/hectare. For all his top châteaux he uses a mix of regular barriques and "cigar"-shaped barrels. They have the same capacity but have a longer, flatter shape. "We wanted to have a flat barrel to increase contact with the lees, this is as close as we could get." The shape also increases the proportion of the wood that is toasted. It goes without saying that all the barriques are new.

Grapes are fully destemmed, but go into the vats without crushing. This is intended to produce some carbonic maceration (fermentation within the berry). Combining the vinification with the aging, achieves the aim of making the wines more approachable. "We wanted to get a creamier palate," Jean-Philippe says. La Confession shows the typical style of the house: a smooth palate of black fruits with tannins receding into the background. Croix St. Georges is a touch more structured, Cap St. George is a little spicier.

Château La Conseillante

***

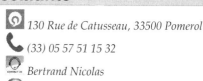

130 Rue de Catusseau, 33500 Pomerol

(33) 05 57 51 15 32

Bertrand Nicolas

contact@la-conseillante.com

www.laconseillante.fr

Pomerol

Duo de Conseillante

12 ha; 45,000 bottles

[map p. 30]

La Conseillante has been owned by the Nicolas family since 1871 (not related to the wine merchants). It's had the same 12 ha for three centuries, but there was a small addition of 0.3 ha in 2015. Vineyards are on gravel soils adjacent to St Emilion; actually a third of the vineyards are in St. Emilion. A new cuverie was constructed in 2012, and the striking circular vat room is full of concrete vats of varying sizes.

Plantings have been 80% Merlot and 20% Cabernet Franc since the 1990s (previously there was more Cabernet Franc). "La Conseillante is not entirely typical of Pomerol, which is known for power and richness; we are known for elegance and silky tannins. We can mix in one bottle the roundness of Pomerol and Merlot with the elegance of Cabernet Franc. We don't want to compete for the biggest wine of the vintage, we want to preserve our elegance, and the silky tannins. That's why we are not considered to be a Parker wine," said winemaker Jean-Michel Laporte.

Cabernet Franc is mostly planted on gravel, and Merlot on clay, but there is some Merlot on gravel. "I think a lot of people only realized the importance of Cabernet Franc a few years ago, but at La Conseillante we've always known its importance. I could have 60% Merlot to 40% Cabernet Franc to match the soils, but I'm very happy with Merlot on gravel, it's very elegant."

Michel Rolland became consulting oenologist in 2013, and Marielle Cazaux took over as estate manager in 2015. No doubt it's due largely to the gravel, but I've always found La Conseillante to be one of the most elegant wines of Pomerol; although it's more Merlot than Cabernet in style, it's well structured, and never goes to excess. Whether this will now change remains to be seen, but Jean-Valmy Nicolas says, "Michel Rolland is helping us to express the potential of La Conseillante, not to change our DNA."

Château Dassault   *

1 Couperie, 33330 St. Emilion

(33) 05 57 55 10 00

Laurence Brun

contact@dassaultwineestates.com

www.dassaultwineestates.com

St. Emilion

D de Dassault

24 ha; 120,000 bottles
[map p. 31]

"We produce the wine at Dassault to lay down for 10-15 years. Dassault is not a blockbuster wine, we don't have clay or limestone, we want to keep the flavor and fruity aromatics. We want elegance more than muscle," says wine-maker Romain Depons.

Dassault originated when Marcel Dassault of the aerospace company purchased Château Couperie in 1955 and renamed it. Vineyards and cellars were renovated. The winery is a workmanlike facility set in a park of 5 ha around the old château, which is farther back. Château Dassault became a grand cru classé in 1969.

Continuous expansion has made Dassault one of the larger landholders in St. Emilion. Marcel's grandson Laurent Dassault purchased neighboring Château La Fleur, just to the north, in 2002; with 6.5 ha, it is much smaller than Dassault, and has remained independent. Château Faurie de Souchard, which has 13 ha just the other side of the road from Dassault, was added to the portfolio in 2014. The 16 ha of Château Trimolet were added in 2016 and incorporated into La Fleur. Altogether there are 70 ha in St. Emilion.

Dassault's vineyards are all in a single block. Plantings are 75% Merlot, 20% Cabernet Franc, and 5% Cabernet Sauvignon. "Five years ago we restructured the vineyards, taking out 5 ha. Another 15 ha will be replanted over the next 10 years. Maybe we will have more Cabernet Franc," Romain says. The second wine comes from various sources—"There's no particular rule"—and is usually about 40% of production.

Dassault is regarded as one of the most reliable wines of the appellation. The 2015 is lighter than you might expect from the vintage, 2012 is soft and attractive, and the 2011 became approachable in 2018, with a classic impression in which Cabernet Franc is more evident than Merlot. Elegance of the vintage shows in 2010, while 2009 is quite reserved and classic. The 2003 was smooth and ready in 2018, with a nice savory tang. "Fifteen years old, this is a mature wine for us," Romain says.

Le Dôme ***

33330 St. Emilion

(33) 05 57 84 64 22

Jonathan Maltus

info@maltus.com

www.maltus.com

St. Emilion

6 ha; 25,000 bottles

Since arriving from Britain twenty years ago, Jonathan Maltus has become one of the largest landholders in St. Emilion, with the purchase (and expansion) of Château Teyssier followed by Château Laforge, but he offers one of the most direct views of terroir in St. Emilion with his four single vineyard wines. These fall into two pairs, Le Carré and Les Astéries (just over 1 ha each) and Vieux Château Mazerat and Le Dôme (about 4 ha each).

Le Carré and Les Astéries are 200 yards apart; Le Carré was planted in 1956, but the vines at Les Astéries are about 90 years old. Both are 80% Merlot. Le Carré is plush, structured and rich, but Les Astéries is all tension, finer and tighter, with a great sense of precision. "Les Astéries is the least Maltus-like wine I make. Our wines are accused of being North American in style," Jonathan says.

Jonathan bought Vieux Château Mazerat in 2008; it's surrounded on three sides by Canon, on the fourth by Angelus. Le Dôme, which used to be part of Vieux Château Mazerat, was purchased previously in 1996. "It's the biggest expression of Cabernet Franc in Bordeaux," Jonathan says. (Plantings are 75% Cabernet Franc.) Vieux Château Mazerat can start off quite stern, with a fine-grained structure waiting for tannins to resolve. Le Dôme is more supple and elegant, with that taut, filigree impression of Cabernet Franc; it takes several years for complexity to emerge. In addition to St. Emilion, Jonathan also makes wine in California and Australia.

Château La Dominique   *

CHÂTEAU
LA DOMINIQUE

GRAND CRU CLASSÉ
SAINT-ÉMILION

Vignobles Clément Fayat
Appellation Saint-Emilion Grand Cru Contrôlée

1 Lieu-Dit La Dominique, 33330 St. Emilion

(33) 05 57 51 31 36

Camille Poupon

contact@vignobles.fayat.com

www.vignobles-fayat.com

St. Emilion

Relais de la Dominique

29 ha; 130,000 bottles
[map p. 31]

The château is famous for the futuristic expansion of its cuverie, with the restaurant Terrasse Rouge on the roof (with views over adjacent Cheval Blanc towards Petrus in Pomerol), which was completed in 2014. Well into oenotourism, there is a spacious tasting room and boutique. The old château is somewhat hidden behind.

La Dominique was the first estate purchased in Bordeaux by the Fayat family, in 1969, when it had only 16 ha. Subsequent purchases included several properties in Pomerol, and Clément-Pichon in the Médoc. The most recent purchase was the adjacent 5 ha estate of Vieux Fortin, which has now been incorporated into La Dominique.

The château is in the middle of the vineyards, which are a single block running from the north to the border with Pomerol at the south. Vineyards are planted with almost 90% Merlot, but replanting is increasing the proportion of Cabernet Franc. There is also a little Cabernet Sauvignon.

Vinification is conventional except that 10-15% is fermented directly in barrel. Grand vin and second wine are both usually close to 90% Merlot. The second wine comes from younger plots, under 25 years, while the grand vin comes from the older plots, up to 45 years (after which plots are replanted). Both age in 60% new oak, the rest being 1-year and 2-year, but the second wine has 10% aged in cuve.

The second wine follows the style of the grand vin but is lighter. The grand vin is decidedly modern. The 2009 is surprisingly savory, but the 2010 shows the full force of the modern approach. I wouldn't quite call the 2014 flashy, but it's very modern in its deep, spicy, black fruits; 2015 is well structured. A grand cru classé since 1955, the château has not yet attained its objective of promotion to premier grand cru classé. Michel Rolland in the consulting winemaker.

Château L'Église Clinet

**

1 Chemin de l'Ancienne Église, 33500 Pomerol

(33) 05 57 25 96 59

Denis Durantou

denis@durantou.com

www.eglise-clinet.com

Pomerol

La Petite Eglise

6 ha; 25,000 bottles
[map p. 30]

This property originated in 1882 as a joint venture merging plots from Clos l'Église and Château Clinet. The wines were sold as Clos l'Église Clinet until the name changed to Château l'Église Clinet in 1954. Until 1983, when Denis Durantou took over, the property was part of a family holding with other agricultural interests, and was managed by Pierre Lasserre of Château Clos René on a profit-sharing arrangement. The wine is typically 85% Merlot and 15% Cabernet Franc. The property got off unusually lightly from the great winter freeze of 1956, and so has a greater proportion of old vines than is common in Pomerol.

Denis has a slightly unusual attitude towards winemaking: harvesting is relatively early, bunches are selected in the vineyard but there is no sorting at the winery, and special tanks are used for fermentation to increase contact between juice and cap. There is no second wine here (La Petite Église is sometimes incorrectly described as the second wine, but is based on a blend of lots from young vines and purchased grapes). The result is a wine that does not go to the extremes of opulence that often characterize Pomerol: I often find a slightly mentholated quality that gives an impression the wine came from a cooler year than was really the case. Well structured for Pomerol, the wine supports long aging: the 1952 (made well before the Durantou era, of course) was still lively in 2014. There's a definite sense of grip to the style.

Château L'Évangile ***

2 Chemin de Maillet, 33500 Pomerol

(33) 05 57 55 45 55

Jean-Pascal Vazart

levangile@lafite.com

www.lafite.com

Pomerol

Blason de l'Évangile

22 ha; 60,000 bottles
[map p. 30]

Lying between Châteaux Petrus and Cheval Blanc, l'Évangile occupies prime terroir of iron-rich clay and gravel. One of the oldest properties in Pomerol, it dates back to 1741. At the start of the twentieth century, it was considered one of the top estates in Pomerol. From 1862, the property was owned by the Ducasse family, until Château Lafite Rothschild acquired a major share in 1990. The vineyards were renovated and a second wine was introduced.

The Rothschilds did not gain full control until a few years later, when they purchased the remaining share, after which they built a new winery (completed in 2004). Greater distinction is now made between parts of the vineyard with differing terroirs, there's more sorting, and new oak has increased to 100%. The vineyards were more or less constant for two hundred years, until in 2012 the Rothschilds purchased an additional 6 ha from neighboring Château Croix de Gay: most of the production from the extra land goes into the second wine, but around 1 ha is added to the grand vin.

L'Évangile has always been an opulent wine, and under the Rothschilds the opulence has become even more overt. The contrast between the 2000 and 2005 vintages is striking: the 2000 is not the blockbuster you might expect from the reputation of the vintage, but is still quite tight, with a sense of tense black fruits. The 2005 is full of high-toned aromatics that would not be out of place on a cult Cabernet from Napa.

Château Figeac ***

Figeac, 33330 St. Emilion

(33) 05 57 24 72 26

Stanislas Aramon

chateau-figeac@chateau-figeac.com

www.chateau-figeac.com

St. Emilion

Petit Figeac

39 ha; 200,000 bottles

[map p. 31]

Until the nineteenth century, Figeac was an enormous estate, extending from St. Emilion into Pomerol. Several of today's famous châteaux lie on parts of the original estate, including neighboring Cheval Blanc, and La Conseillante in Pomerol. The estate came by marriage to the Manoncourt family in 1892, and into the hands of Thierry Manoncourt in 1947. Since then, Figeac has been regarded as one of the top châteaux of St. Emilion; at the top of Premier Grand Cru Classé B, its official standing was just below the two châteaux (Cheval Blanc and Ausone) classified as group A.

With its equal proportions of Cabernet Sauvignon, Cabernet Franc, and Merlot, Figeac is sui generis, without doubt the right bank's leader in Cabernet Sauvignon. Perhaps fashion has partly overtaken Figeac with the rise of the extremely lush style of modern St. Emilion, as in the reclassification of 2012, Pavie and l'Angélus were promoted over Figeac into class A. Thierry's son-in-law, Eric d'Aramon, who managed the estate at the time, said, "We are not looking for high alcohol. I was the latest to pick 20-30 years ago, now I'm in the average." Although current vintages are more approachable than those of the past, this is still a wine that benefits more from age than other St. Emilion's. The 1966 showed a brilliant delicacy in 2014.

Eric was replaced in a family coup in 2013, and it remains to be seen whether the subsequent appointment of Michel Rolland as consultant will change Figeac's unique style. The château is now undertaking an extensive program of renovation, and it will not be possible to visit until this is finished in 2020.

Château La Fleur de Boüard *

12 Bertineau, 33500 Néac

(33) 05 57 25 25 13

Hubert de Boüard

contact@lafleurdebouard.com

www.lafleurdebouard.com

Lalande-de-Pomerol

Château la Fleur St. Georges

25 ha; 100,000 bottles
[map p. 29]

One of the most influential people in St. Emilion, Hubert Boüard has fingers in many pies. He has seen Château Angélus promoted to Premier Grand Cru Classé A, also owns Château Bellevue in St. Emilion, and is a consulting oenologist for more than 60 other châteaux. He purchased La Fleur de Boüard from an insurance company in 1998. Plantings are 80% Merlot (with 15% Cabernet Franc and 5% Cabernet Sauvignon), but that is more or less the only thing that is typical about the château relative to Lalande de Pomerol in general.

Fleur de Boüard has its own winemaking team, and a modern gravity-feed winery. Technique is somewhat different from Angélus, using délestage (rack and return) with tronconique tanks, producing a wine that is soft and rich. It matures for 12-33 months in barriques including 75% new oak. The supercuvée, Le Plus de Boüard, only 3-4,000 bottles, was made for the first time in 2000. It's based on selection; "even during one pass through the vineyards there is selection between Fleur and Plus," says Laurent Benoît at Angélus.

Fleur de Boüard is extremely powerful for Lalande de Pomerol, with forward black fruits, smoky aromatics, and lots of evident new oak. It needs quite a long time to calm down. Le Plus is the same squared (only the 2000 is at all ready now). These are by far the most expensive wines of the appellation, but whether they are the best depends on what you want from Lalande de Pomerol.

Château La Fleur-Pétrus   ***

7 rue de Tropchaud, 33500 Pomerol

(33) 05 57 51 78 96

Geneviève Sandifer

info@jpmoueix.com

www.moueix.com

Pomerol

19 ha; 50,000 bottles
[map p. 30]

La Fleur Petrus was the first property Jean-Pierre Moueix purchased, in 1950. The property is named for the original vineyard block, lying between Château Lafleur and Petrus. There are two other major plots, one between Le Pin and Trotanoy, the other just outside the town. In 2013, the cuverie was moved from the original château near Petrus to a building opposite the church in Pomerol (it's the original Presbytery of the church), on a block purchased in 2005. This places it more or less in the center of the vineyard holdings.

The vineyard area has roughly doubled since Moueix's original purchase, and the style of Fleur Petrus has evolved as additional blocks were purchased; 4 ha were bought from Le Gay in 1995, and the most recent block came in 2009 from Château Guyot. The vineyards have three types of soil: light clay at the new château, heavier clay near Petrus, and gravel terroir near Trotanoy. The impression at the new château is workmanlike rather than glitzy, with concrete vats and a practical barrel room. "La Fleur Petrus is probably the lightest of the Moueix properties," says export manager Frédéric Lospied.

Winemaking is traditional and moderate, with up to 50% new oak for 14-20 months depending on the vintage. The blend is typical for Pomerol, with 80-90% Merlot, but the style is not at all heavy: it can give quite an elegant impression, with a good sense of freshness. Following general Moueix policy, there is no second wine.

Château Fombrauge *

📍 *Saint Christophe-des-Bardes, St. Emilion, 33330*

📞 *(33) 05 57 24 77 12*

Nicolas Contiero

@ *visiteschateaux@pape-clement.com*

🌐 *www.fombrauge.com*

St. Emilion

🚜 *58 ha; 200,000 bottles*
[map p. 32]

The rather grand property of Château Fombrauge, with its long history, was only a Grand Cru in St. Emilion until it was promoted to Grand Cru Classé in 2012. To what extent this reflects the improvements in the wine brought about since Bernard Magrez purchased the estate in 1999, and to what extent it represents glory reflected from Magrez-Fombrauge is hard to determine. Somewhat of a specialist in reviving under-performing châteaux, Bernard made considerable investments in replanting the vineyards, renovating the chais, and generally improving the property.

Château Fombrauge is located at Saint Christophe des Bardes, where the soils are calcareous clay, but also has vineyards to the southeast at Saint Etienne de Lisse on limestone and molasses, and then vineyards at Saint Hippolyte, with more of a clay terroir.

Magrez-Fombrauge started as a micro-cuvée in 2000, when the best lots were selected from three plots (producing only 6,000 bottles). Similar "Cuvées d'Exception" are made, each in tiny amounts, from several of Magrez's properties, but Magrez-Fombrauge has become independent. "It was a cuvée but now it's a different Château, it's not vinified at Fombrauge," Bernard explains. Some 2.4 ha at Saint Hippolyte now provide the basis for Magrez-Fombrauge.

While Château Fombrauge has the style of a typical St. Emilion, Magrez-Fombrauge has the high extraction, richness, and alcohol, of a garage wine. All Magrez wines are modern, but this is über-modern.

Château Fontenil *

 11 Lieu-dit Cardeneau, 33141 Saillans

📞 (33) 05 57 51 23 05

 Michel Rolland

@ contact@rollandcollection.com

🌐 www.rollandcollection.com

 Fronsac

 9 ha; 40,000 bottles
[map p. 28]

This property has been owned since 1986 by Michel Rolland, the famous flying winemaker who advises many châteaux on the Right Bank. Purchased as a country home, the property came with vineyards on the typical terroir of clay over limestone. With Michel's expertise, Château Fontenil probably makes the best wine in Fronsac, a satellite of Pomerol.

But the château's fame comes as much from an incident in 2000, when Michel decided to protect the vines from rain by placing plastic sheeting between the rows, so the water would run off instead of soaking the roots. INAO was not amused, and refused to allow the wine to have the appellation label, so it was declassified to a separate cuvée, called Defi de Fontenil, and labeled as Vin de France. (A similar incident at Château Valandraud led to the creation of Interdit de Valandraud.) Because the best plots in the vineyard were protected, Defi de Fontenil became a special cuvée. The technique was so effective—"the grapes were considerably sweeter with more advanced maturity," Michel says—that it was repeated it in 2001 and 2004.

Coming from the same plots, and still labeled as Vin de France, Defi de Fontenil has become the flagship cuvée (although plastic sheeting is not usually used); a notch below, Château Fontenil remains in the Fronsac AOP. How do they compare? Both start with overt fruits, but Fontenil closes up to become more classic in mid life, while Defi de Fontenil has greater warmth and aromatic complexity.

Château Fougas

CHÂTEAU
FOUGAS

Maldoror

2007

GRAND VIN DE BORDEAUX
JEAN-YVES BECHET

Fougas, 33710 Lansac

(33) 05 57 68 42 15

Jean Yves Bechet

jean-yves.bechet@wanadoo.fr

www.fougas.com

Côtes de Bourg

17 ha; 80,000 bottles
[map p. 28]

Jean-Yves Bechet bought Château Fougas in 1976, and in 1993 started to produce the Maldoror cuvée from a single hectare; it was only 10% of production. The estate was converted to biodynamic viticulture, quality improved, and slowly Maldoror was increased to its present proportion, about 90% of production. The "regular" cuvée is called the Prestige. In effect Maldoror has gone from a special cuvée to becoming the grand vin.

Maldoror's proportion of 25% Cabernet Sauvignon is more or less constant each year; the Cabernet vines are now about forty years old, which no doubt contributes to the quality. "Cabernet Sauvignon is difficult here, but when we get ripe Cabernet Sauvignon, its taste is extraordinary, with lots of structure," says Jean-Yves. I don't think I would describe the wine as claret, because it doesn't quite have that tang of dominant Cabernet Sauvignon, but it seems more like a half way house between right bank and left bank than a typical right bank wine. The wine is matured for up to eighteen months in 50% new oak.

There's good structure with the fruits, although there isn't quite the power of the Cabernet Sauvignon-dominated wines of the Médoc. "If you like powerful wines, drink between three and seven years, if not they will age much longer," is Jean-Yves's view. Certainly the wine ages well; tertiary development starts after a decade, and the inaugural vintage was just beginning to fade gently in 2012. This is one of the top wines of the Côtes de Bourg.

Clos Fourtet ★★

1 Chatelet Sud, 33330 St. Emilion

(33) 05 57 24 70 90

Matthieu Cuvelier

closfourtet@closfourtet.com

www.closfourtet.com

St. Emilion

Closerie de Fourtet

20 ha; 75,000 bottles

[map p. 31]

Just outside the town walls, opposite an old entrance to St. Emilion, surrounded by stone walls, Clos Fourtet originated as a fort. Owned successively by negociants Ginestet and Lurton, quality was a bit erratic, until Pierre Lurton (now Director at Cheval Blanc) became winemaker. The estate was purchased in 2001 by Philippe Cuvelier, a businessman enthused by Bordeaux, who later also bought Château Poujeaux in Moulis.

Clos Fourtet's vineyards are in two blocks: the *clos* of 14 ha extends from the town walls to the west; another 6 ha are farther north. The grand vin mostly comes from the first block, which has the classic terroir of a thin layer of clay over limestone. The 6 ha block is not as good, and mostly goes into the second wine. Three other properties in St. Emilion have recently been added to the portfolio: Les Grands Murailles (adjacent to Clos Fourtet), Château Clos St Martin, and Côte de Baleau.

A large part of Clos Fourtet was replanted in 2001, so today the vines are mostly relatively young. Although Merlot is always at least 85%, recent vintages seem to be quite stern when young, with structure more evident than usual for St. Emilion. Most of the rest of the blend is usually Cabernet Sauvignon (typically around 10%), so Cabernet Franc is rarely more than 5%. (Until 1999, the blend was usually only Merlot and Cabernet Sauvignon.) "We try to make the wine with freshness. We are not looking for opulence, we don't want too much extraction," is how Matthieu Cuvelier describes the wine.

Château La Gaffelière ★★

CHÂTEAU
LA GAFFELIÈRE
1ᵉʳ GRAND CRU CLASSÉ
SAINT-ÉMILION GRAND CRU
2004
Comte de Malet Roquefort
PROPRIÉTAIRE
MIS EN BOUTEILLE AU CHÂTEAU

○ La Gaffelière-Ouest, 33330 St. Emilion

☎ (33) 05 57 24 72 15

○ Comte de Malet Roquefort

@ visite@gaffeliere.com

⊕ www.gaffeliere.com

○ St. Emilion

② Clos La Gaffelière

🍇 23 ha; 80,000 bottles

[map p. 31]

"We didn't want to impress visitors, it's not Disneyland here," says Alexandre Malet Roquefort, going around the small winery, renovated in 2013, and packed with equipment including purple fermentation cuves in an interesting conical shape. The Malet Roqueforts have been making wine here since the sixteenth century. One of the most traditional wines in St. Emilion, La Gaffelière was languishing when Alexandre and his father decided to bring it up to speed in 2004. Production was halved, and Stéphane Derenoncourt became consulting oenologist.

Vineyards are around the château, running from the slopes below Ausone to the plain beyond. The Cabernet Sauvignon was taken out in 2005, and a planting program was started in 2006. Cabernet Franc from the bottom of the hill was replaced with Merlot and replanted at the top of the hill. "Previously everyone put the best parcels into Merlot, now we know to make the best wine it's necessary to put the best parcels into Cabernet Franc," Alexandre explains.

Although plantings are 70% Merlot, I have always found Gaffelière to be one of the more restrained wines in St. Emilion. "The DNA of Gaffelière is really classic, it's one of a small group in St. Emilion that didn't change its style in recent years. We like wine that is fruity, not too extracted. The style of Gaffelière should not change with me or my children. I want them to realize they must make wine as it should be, not as they would like it to be." The revival is well under way.

Château Le Gay

11 Chemin de Chantecaille, 33500 Pomerol

(33) 05 57 25 34 34

Henri Parent

communication@montviel.com

www.vignoblespereverge.com

Pomerol

Manoir de Gay

11 ha; 20,000 bottles

[map p. 30]

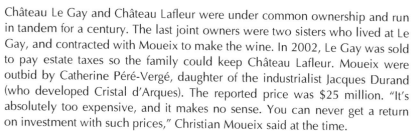

Château Le Gay and Château Lafleur were under common ownership and run in tandem for a century. The last joint owners were two sisters who lived at Le Gay, and contracted with Moueix to make the wine. In 2002, Le Gay was sold to pay estate taxes so the family could keep Château Lafleur. Moueix were outbid by Catherine Péré-Vergé, daughter of the industrialist Jacques Durand (who developed Cristal d'Arques). The reported price was $25 million. "It's absolutely too expensive, and it makes no sense. You can never get a return on investment with such prices," Christian Moueix said at the time.

Catherine Péré-Vergé already owned Château Montviel, a less well-known Pomerol, and also added Château La Violette, a tiny property of 1.3 ha of 50-year-old Merlot between Trotanoy and Le Pin, as well as châteaux in Lalande-de-Pomerol and a bodega in Argentina. There was a massive program of investment at Le Gay, with a new winery constructed next to the old house, and some additional vineyards planted (on one of the few remaining unplanted plots in Pomerol, near Lafleur). After Catherine died in 2013, her son, Henri Parent, took over.

"We like to be discrete," they say at Château le Gay, explaining why the property has no identification outside, making it hard to find. But the wines are flamboyant. The vineyards at Le Gay fall into two parts: those higher up, to the north, are used for Le Gay; those lower down, to the south, are used for Manoir de Gay, which is not so much a second wine as an alternative from different plots, as vinification is the same as Le Gay. La Gay is 90% Merlot and 10% Cabernet Franc.

Vinification for Le Gay, Manoir, and La Violette is idiosyncratic: they call it micro-vinification as it takes place in barriques. Invented by consultant Michel

Rolland, this started for La Violette in 2006, and was extended to all three wines in 2014, after the construction of a new cuverie with a temperature-controlled vat room. "We cannot control temperature in the barrel, so we control the room," says manager Vincent Bernard. What difference does this make? "Well, every plot is different, there are only 150 vines per barrel. The wine has a better balance with the oak. With conventional vinification there can be a disjunction between the wine and the oak, here it is much better integrated." All three wines use exclusively new oak. It would be fair to call Le Gay an arch-modernist.

Château Gazin ★★

 1 chemin de Chantecuille, 33500 Pomerol

 (33) 05 57 51 07 05

 Nicolas de Bailliencourt

 contact@gazin.com

 www.gazin.com

 Pomerol

 L'Hospitalet de Gazin

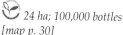 *24 ha; 100,000 bottles*
[map p. 30]

Gazin is an old-line Pomerol château, owned by the de Bailliencourt family since 1917, and run by Nicolas de Bailliencourt since 1989. The estate was supposedly the site of a hospital built by knights for pilgrims in the twelfth century. The estate is the one of the largest in Pomerol, and has a real château. Wine production started in the second half of the nineteenth century. The winery consists of a series of practical buildings around the château.

Gazin was originally larger, but 4.5 ha were sold to neighboring Petrus in 1970; only a narrow track separates the vineyards from Petrus. Two thirds of the vineyards are on the plateau of Pomerol, with clay and limestone soils. Plantings are 90% Merlot, 6% Cabernet Franc, and 4% Cabernet Sauvignon. The proportion of Cabernets in the wine has varied from almost 20% to zero (the 2012 was 100% Merlot). There have been ups and downs in quality. Reputation was high in the 1950s, declined in the sixties through eighties, and then revived in the 1990s after Nicolas took over.

The approach is traditional, with vinification in concrete vats. Half the grand vin has MLF in barrique, everything else has MLF in vat. The grand vin ages half in new barriques and half in 1-year barriques; the second wine ages in 1-3-year barriques. Based on selection before aging, the second wine is usually 15% of production, but has been as high as 45%.

"Half new oak is enough for us," says Nicolas de Bailliencourt, "We don't want to make blockbuster wines, we want to make wines with finesse. Finesse is the most difficult thing to achieve in a wine." Aided by a new winemaker, there has been a move in this direction. The 2009 is straightforward and somewhat sturdy, 2010 has more of a taut backbone, 2011 is rich but a little superficial, 2012 is a touch herbal, 2014 is a little sweeter and riper than most this year, and 2015 achieves a sophisticated impression of purity and refinement. In the past I have felt the wines should be drunk within 5-15 years of the vintage, but the 2015 shows a move towards greater ageworthiness.

Château Gombaude Guillot *

4 Les Grandes Vignes, 33500 Pomerol

(33) 05 57 51 17 40

Olivier Laval

gombaude@free.fr

www.chateau-gombaude-guillot.com

Pomerol

Cadet de Gombaude

7 ha; 35,000 bottles

[map p. 30]

The property is located just down the street from the church at Pomerol. The family has been here since 1860 and is now in the sixth generation; Olivier Laval started in 2006. The grand vin comes from a plot of 4 ha around the winery, and the second wine comes from two or three other plots. The mix of grape varieties is more or less the same for both wines, 65% Merlot, 30% Cabernet Franc, and 5% Malbec (some of the Malbec is very old).

The vat room is on the upper level of the small winery, and the barrel room below gives a somewhat higgledy-piggledy impression. Vinification is idiosyncratic, partly in new barriques, and partly in cuve, but there is an air of experimentation. In addition to barriques, amphora are used for aging. "We feel they give a more open wine," Olivier explains.

Tasting samples of the current vintage, the cuve gives a bright, ripe impression. Barriques give a slightly stern impression with more sense of structure. Amphora show somewhere between the barrique and cuve, with a lovely balance, and indeed make a more open impression. "The wine evolves more rapidly in amphora, so it's moved between the different types of containers during aging," Olivier says.

Bottled wines show as opulent and very Pomerol-ish from top vintages, tautter and moving in a savory direction from lesser vintages. Olivier has been reducing sulfur. "It's less than 25 mgm in 2015. So it's basically a natural wine," he says.

In addition to the grand vin and second wine, there's another cuvée with the unusual grape mix of two thirds Merlot and one third Malbec. This is PomNRoll, which started as an experiment in 2010, and has been produced since 2011. It's bright and lively, and easy to drink.

Château Grand Corbin-Despagne   *

D244, 33330 St. Emilion

(33) 05 57 51 08 38

François Despagne

contact@grand-corbin-despagne.com

www.grand-corbin-despagne.com

St. Emilion

Petit Corbin Despagne

29 ha; 125,000 bottles
[map p. 31]

Part of what was the Grand Corbin estate in the fifteenth century, located in the northwest near the border with Pomerol, Château Grand Corbin-Despagne was a grand cru classé in the original classification in 1955. It was demoted in 1996 and reinstated in 2006. The Despagne family bought it after the French Revolution, and François has been in charge since 1996. He also owns Château Le Chemin in Pomerol, and established Château Ampélia in Castillon (see mini-profile) in 2000, because he wanted to create his own estate.

"I am the seventh generation, I went to university to study science, then I did research with Denis Dubourdieu, but in 1996 my family asked if I would come back and I returned here. All my studies were on yeast but now I do experiments in the vineyards," François says. "I've done a soil map, so I can match grape varieties to soils to be more precise." Plantings are 75% Merlot, 24% Cabernet Franc, and 1% Cabernet Sauvignon. His scientific background shows in the experiment he has underway to use biodynamics on a 6 ha plot to compare it with organic viticulture.

The grand vin comes from vines more than 20 years old, and the second wine comes from vines of 20-20 years old, but there is also some selection. There is a third wine from deselected lots, just labeled as St. Emilion. "It is not signed with the name of château," François says, emphasizing his determination to maintain its reputation.

If I were to use a single word to describe the style it would be polished. Grand Corbin Despagne has a smooth sheen that becomes almost unctuous in a top vintage and shows as tautness in lesser vintages. Ampelia follows the same style. Petit Corbin Despagne is a lighter version of the grand vin. The Pomerol, a 100% Merlot from a 1 ha plot, is softer and more chocolaty.

"I can't make the best wine in the world but I want to make the best wine possible from my terroir," François says. The 2010 is smooth and scarcely developed yet, 2012 does not have the pizzazz of 2010 but shows that refined house style, 2014 is more structured, and 2015 has that polished sheen.

Château Hosanna ***

Jean-Pierre Moueix, 54, Quai du Priourat, B.p. 129, 33500 Libourne

(33) 05 57 51 78 96

Christian Moueix

info@jpmoueix.com

www.moueix.com

Pomerol

5 ha; 18,000 bottles

There is no château, only vineyards. One of the newest properties in Pomerol, Château Hosanna owes its origin to the deconstruction of Château Certan-Giraud after it was purchased by Moueix. The best vineyards were split off to become Château Hosanna in 1999, 4 ha were sold to Château Nénin, and the rump became Château Certan-Marzelle.

The terroir is essentially red gravel with a base of clay and *casse de fer,* and a drainage system was installed to satisfy concerns that water had been a problem. The vines are middle aged, with an average around 40 years. "Hosanna is unusual for Moueix; with 30% Cabernet Franc it's the highest. The goal was to make the Cheval Blanc of Pomerol," says Frédéric Lospied of Moueix, but he's quick to add, "this is a joke." (However, you might consider that the choice of the name Hosanna implies a certain ambition for the wine.)

Would you consider Château Hosanna to be a garage wine, I asked? "That would be pejorative. We would agree with the distinction that Château La Fleur Petrus is an assemblage of terroirs but Hosanna is a single vineyard wine." The Moueix view is that Hosanna's high content of Cabernet Franc makes it a more feminine wine than Petrus or Trotanoy. The wine is matured in 50% new oak for 18 months. It's been made every year from 1999 to 2012, but there was no production in 2013 because yields were simply too low. Hosanna is always very expensive, if not yet a rival to Petrus.

Château Lafleur   ***

4 Chemin de Chantecaille, 33500 Pomerol

(33) 05 57 84 44 03

Jacques Guinaudeau

(33) 05 57 84 83 31

www.chateau-lafleur.fr

Pomerol

Les Pensées de Lafleur

5 ha; 20,000 bottles

[map p. 30]

This tiny property has a reputation in inverse proportion to its size. In the same family since it was founded in 1872 by the proprietor of Château Le Gay, it was previously owned by two sisters who lived at Le Gay. The wine was made by Moueix until the sisters leased the property to their nephew Jacques Guinaudeau in 1985, and then in 2002 Jacques purchased it. The "château" is a somewhat obscure farmhouse with a tiny vineyard adjoining Petrus.

There is surprising variation in terroir for such a small property, from gravel over clay to sandy gravel. Pensées de Lafleur started as a second wine in 1987, but since 1995 has come 90% from a lower strip of deeper soils running along the southwest edge of the vineyard. "A large part of our identity comes from the high proportion of Cabernet Franc," says Baptiste Guinaudeau. Usually about 55% Cabernet Franc, Lafleur has a restrained character distinct from the average Pomerol.

The focus in winemaking is to avoid too much extraction. "We don't use the word extraction, we want to infuse," says Baptiste. "Cuvaison is only 12-15 days, which is short for Bordeaux, because the wine is already well structured." Élevage sees some restraint. "We love barrels but we hate oak; 80% is aged in 6-month barrels, the rest is new oak." This is old-fashioned Bordeaux in the best sense—elegant rather than powerful or jammy, with moderate alcohol and restrained wood. The Guinaudeaus also make wine at Grand Village in Fronsac.

Château Larcis Ducasse *

📍 1 Grottes d'Arsis, 33330 St. Laurent-des-Combes

📞 (33) 05 57 24 70 84

👤 Nicolas Thienpont

@ contact@larcis-ducasse.com

🌐 www.larcis-ducasse.com

▦ St. Emilion

🚫 📊

🚜 10 ha; 28,000 bottles

[map p. 31]

Larcis Ducasse has belonged to the same family since 1813, but as they are absentee owners, everything depends on the management. The wine was a reliable, if not very exciting, representation of St. Emilion at the Grand Cru Classé level until Nicolas Thienpont was asked to take over in 2002. More detailed attention paid off, and the château was promoted to Premier Grand Cru Classé in the reclassification of 2012.

The facility itself seems a little old-fashioned, but was ahead of its time, as it took advantage of the slope to build a natural gravity feed system. Cement cuves are underneath grape reception, and élevage lasts 14-17 months in 60% new oak, using both barriques and 500 liter barrels (for lots from the warmest plots). Vineyards are located in prime terroir, with 15% of the plots on the limestone plateau, and the rest descending down terraces on the Côte Pavie slope to the south, with very calcareous terroir of molasses of white clay.

"Going up the terraces, there's a distinct change of character. Merlot is not the same on each terrace. There's a contrast between the spot, which is warm, and the soil, which is cool. So we get good ripeness but at the same time keep freshness. There's good aromatic complexity but good acidity also," is how winemaker David Suire describes the situation. This is not a flamboyant example of St. Emilion; the wine is on the reserved side, in cooler vintages showing an almost savory or herbal touch, which in warmer vintages shows as minerality.

Château Latour à Pomerol   ***

Jean-Pierre Moueix, 54, Quai du Priourat, B.p. 129, 33500 Libourne

(33) 05 57 51 78 96

Geneviève Sandifer

info@jpmoueix.com

www.moueix.com

Pomerol

8 ha; 30,000 bottles
[map p. 30]

For many years under the same ownership as Petrus, this small estate has remained unchanged since it took its present form after the division of the Chambaud estate in 1917, when it was inherited by Mme. Edmond Loubat (who later acquired Petrus). She added some vineyards, and in due course, in 1961, Latour à Pomerol and Petrus passed to her niece, Lily Lacoste. Mme Lacoste sold her stake in Petrus to Moueix, but kept Latour à Pomerol until 2002, when she donated it to a Catholic charity. However, since 1962 it has been managed by Moueix; as now there is no owner with an interest in wine production, to all intents and purposes today this is another estate in the Moueix portfolio.

The vineyards lie in two separate areas, with 5 ha consisting of gravel soil on a clay subsoil, in the best area close to the church of Pomerol, the rest elsewhere on lighter, sandier soils. (There isn't much information about the history of these parcels before they became Latour à Pomerol.) The rather gracious château is on the main parcel, Les Grandes Vignes, and takes its name from a tower at one end of the building. Vines have an average age of forty years. The wine is a typical Pomerol with 90% Merlot, matured for 18 months in 50% new barriques. Given the small scale of production, there is no second wine. The grand vin is full-bodied, ripe, and rich, opulent and powerful rather than elegant, needing time to develop, but lasting for up to thirty years.

La Mondotte

***

LA MONDOTTE

Comtes von Neipperg
2008

⊙ *33330 St. Emilion*

📞 *(33) 05 57 24 71 33*

👤 *Stephan von Neipperg*

@ *info@neipperg.com*

🌐 *www.neipperg.com*

◉ *St. Emilion*

🏭 *5 ha; 12,000 bottles*

Is La Mondotte a garage wine, I asked Stephan von Neipperg? "I never understood why they call it a garage wine," he says. "La Mondotte has been completely independent since 1996. It is now a classified growth. You cannot talk about a first growth being a garage wine." Its independence is almost an accident. "I tried to bring La Mondotte into Canon La Gaffelière in the classification of 1996, but they told me, it's different, you have to see if you can age fifteen years. Well, now we have shown it."

Whereas Canon La Gaffelière is at the foot of the town, La Mondotte is well to the east on the limestone plateau. The vines are 65-100 years old; some are even on their own roots by marcottage from grafted vines. Following the rejection in the classification of 1996, a cuverie was constructed on the property, and the wine was vinified separately. It now has the same classification as Canon La Gaffelière!

The similarity to the garage wines lies in the tiny scale of production and the intensity, the sheer richness, of the wine, with deep black fruits on the palate, cut by chocolaty tannins, very much the iron fist in the velvet glove. The wine is aged entirely in 100% new oak. Yet with a quarter Cabernet Franc to the three quarters Merlot, it avoids the jammy quality of some garage wines and remains a real wine, albeit on the powerful side for St. Emilion. You have to wonder what would have happened if La Mondotte had in fact been incorporated into Canon La Gaffelière.

Château Nénin **

 66 Route de Montagne, Nenin, 33500 Libourne

 (33) 05 57 51 00 01

 Jules Biessy

 contact@leoville-las-cases.com

 www.domaines-delon.com

 Pomerol

 La Fugue de Nénin

 32 ha; 110,000 bottles
[map p. 30]

The second-largest estate in Pomerol, with a high reputation in the late nineteenth century, Château Nénin was a distinct under-performer by the time the Despujol's, who had owned it since 1847, sold it to their cousins, the Delons of Château Léoville-Lascases, in 1997. "Nothing was done here for 30 years," says export manager Antoine Gimbert. The best that could be said is that the wine was somewhat four-square.

Unusually for Pomerol, the château is quite grand, with a surrounding park. Winemaking facilities are in buildings around the château. Just north of the village of Catusseau, the vineyards lie around the château, with soils of sand-clay on a subsoil of *casse de fer*, and were restructured immediately after the purchase, with significant replanting, especially to replace vines that had been planted on poor rootstocks after the great freeze of 1956. Cabernet Franc has been increased. Drainage systems were installed, manual harvesting replaced machine harvesting, and the winery was modernized. The vineyards were expanded by acquiring 4 ha in 1999 from Château Certan-Giraud.

The grand vin is 70% Merlot and 30% Cabernet Franc, and ages in 35-40% new oak. "We don't want the wine to suffer from over-oaking or over-extraction," Antoine says. The Delons introduced a second wine, which comes largely from the 18 ha immediately around the château, but it also includes some other declassified lots. This is about two thirds of production. It is 90% Merlot and 10% Cabernet Franc, and ages in 30% new oak.

Improvement in the wine was not instantaneous, but it started to come back on form in the early 2000's. "The first vintage where you really see the new style is 2012," Antoine says, "We want to keep the creamy character without losing Pomerol character." Both second wine and grand vin display a relatively strong structure for Pomerol, giving a powerful impression that needs some time to come around.

Château Pavie ***

Iᵉ GRAND CRU CLASSÉ

Château Pavie
SAINT-ÉMILION GRAND CRU
Appellation Saint-Émilion Grand Cru Contrôlée
2008
G. & G. PERSE   VITICULTEURS

2 Pimpinelle, 33330 St. Emilion

(33) 05 57 55 43 43

Gérard Perse

contact@vignoblesperse.com

www.vignoblesperse.com

St. Emilion

Arômes de Pavie

37 ha; 120,000 bottles
[map p. 31]

When Château Pavie and adjacent Pavie Decesse came on the market in 1997, supermarket magnate Gérard Perse, who had bought Château Monbousquet in 1993, acquired Pavie Decesse. When Pavie had not sold a year later, "He decided to change his life, he sold the supermarkets and left Paris to build up Château Pavie," says Gérard's son-in-law, Henrique da Costa. Since then, it's been a steady upward path, culminating in promotion to Premier Grand Cru Classé A (now engraved in stone over the entrance to the massive new building, which took five years to build).

Inside the new facility are vast vat and barrel rooms, with separate fermenters for each plot. The vineyard is in a single block facing south, running down from the château. Merlot has been decreased from 70% to 60% (now with 25% Cabernet Franc and 15% Cabernet Sauvignon). "This may be the best place in St. Emilion for Cabernet," Henrique says.

The transition to a very lush, extracted, New World style, laden with new oak, since Perse bought Pavie is controversial, generally loved in the U.S. but not in the U.K.; although vintages tasted during my visit seemed more measured, one still questions what this says about Bordeaux. The major part of Pavie Decesse was incorporated into Pavie in 2012, leaving a rump of 3.5 ha (see mini-profile). In addition to owning several châteaux in St. Emilion, Perse Vignobles produces Esprit de Pavie, which is a Bordeaux AOP from the estates in Castillon. Michel Rolland consults for all the châteaux of Vignobles Perse.

Château Pavie Macquin ★★

1 Peygenestau, 33330 St. Emilion

(33) 05 57 24 74 23

Nicolas Thienpont

pavie.macquin@wanadoo.fr

www.pavie-macquin.com

St. Emilion

Les Chênes de Macquin

15 ha; 60,000 bottles
[map p. 31]

Surrounded by limestone terraces, overlooking the grand church at St. Emilion, Pavie Macquin is located right in the heart of the limestone plateau. Access is by a very steep twisting one track path that requires much maneuvering even for small cars. There are old buildings behind and a stylish tasting room in front, built two years ago as an extension of an old maison. Vineyards are all in one holding except for two parcels. Everything in the field of view is part of Pavie Macquin; just over the hill is Pavie.

"Pavie Macquin was on the verge of being declassified under the previous management," says Nicolas Thienpont, who was appointed in 1994 to run the estate for the absentee owners (who are descendants of Albert Macquin). The château has made great strides under Thienpont management, and was promoted to Premier Grand Cru Classé in the reclassification of 2006.

The elevated location means that maturation is slow, and this is always one of the last châteaux to harvest. There is 60% new oak during élevage. I would say that since the reclassification, most vintages show a sense of increased elegance, partly because the wine tastes as though it has more Cabernet Franc than it really does (it's actually 80% Merlot). Winemaker David Suire says there's one area that's planted with Merlot but you would think it was Cabernet Franc from its refinement. "Pavie Macquin has a certain power but is always fresh, we look for grand purity and definition," is Nicolas's view.

Château Petit Village **

126 route de Catusseau, 33500 Pomerol

(33) 05 57 51 21 08

Marine Dejeux

contact@petit-village.com

www.petit-village.com

Pomerol

Le Jardin de Petit-Village

11 ha; 40,000 bottles
[map p. 30]

This property was not exactly neglected during the twentieth century, but it was owned by proprietors who, although located merely on the other side of the Gironde, did not have it at the forefront of their attention. First it was owned by the negociant Ginestet, and then it passed by inheritance to Bruno Prats of Cos d'Estournel. Its revival began when it was sold in 1989 to AXA (owners of Château Pichon Baron in Pauillac and Château Suduiraut in Sauternes). The château was extended into new winery in a rather stark, modern style in 2005.

Located on the gravel plateau that extends from St. Emilion, Petit Village is in a splendid location, with a direct view across to the church at Pomerol. The vineyards are mostly in a single block, occupying a triangle, with Châteaux Le Pin, Vieux Château Certan, and La Conseillante at the apices. The soil is blue clay and *crasse de fer* going towards Pomerol, and more gravelly sloping down to Catusseau. Plantings are 75% Merlot, 17% Cabernet Franc, and 8% Cabernet Sauvignon, with the Cabernets located on the gravelly bottom quarter.

The style here is towards elegance and freshness rather than power or opulence. (This was thought to be partly due to an unusually high proportion of Cabernet Sauvignon, but these were very old vines more recently discovered to be really Cabernet Franc. No doubt the age of the vines contributes in any case to the sense of structure in the wine. The blend in the grand vin is usually close to the plantings, and it ages in 60% new barriques.

The second wine is not very similar to the grand vin. It comes from younger vines and is usually 100% Merlot. The difference was accentuated further when Diana Berrouet-Garcia, the new technical director in 2015, changed the direction of the second wine to look for my juiciness, and basically eliminated new oak in the Jardin.

Petrus ****

 3, Route de Lussac, 33500 Pomerol

 (33) 05 57 51 78 96

 Elisabeth Jaubert

@ *ejaubert@petrus.com*

 Pomerol

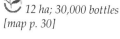 *12 ha; 30,000 bottles*
[map p. 30]

The most famous wine in Pomerol, and often the most expensive wine in Bordeaux, the fame of Petrus goes well back into the twentieth century, when Mme. Edmond Loubert bought shares progressively from 1925 until she became sole owner in 1949. The Moueix involvement started when Jean-Pierre Moueix became sole agent in 1943. He was left a small portion when Mme Loubert died, and in 1964 he bought a majority interest from one of the heirs, subsequently expanded into full control. (Moueix point out that, contrary to popular impression, Petrus does not have an accent on the "e").

The "château" was famously shabby, but was renovated about five years ago to become quite showy. It sits on an oval-shaped hill with shallow topsoil over deep blue clay—the famous buttonhole where the clay comes close to the surface. Its ability to store up water in the winter gives a good reserve for the summer and is part of Petrus's unique character. "On this soil the Merlot develops a high degree of tannins, but they are not aggressive," says Elisabeth Jaubert at the château. There was a small section of Cabernet Franc from 1957-2010, but now the wine is 100% Merlot.

Grapes are destemmed and cooled on arrival, fermented in concrete, transferred to stainless steel for malolactic, and then into barriques, with about 50% new oak. Vinification is by plot, but plots are defined by vine age. "Obviously we don't make Petrus from 100% of the grapes. The last time that happened was 1975," Elisabeth says, "but there will no second wine." Usually about 70% of the crop goes into Petrus, but rumors surfaced again in 2017 that the remainder would be put into a second wine instead of being sold off. The combination of power and elegance is sui generis, so it's unclear how that might play in a second wine.

Le Pin   ***

Les Grands Champs, Rue la Fontaine, 33500 Pomerol

(33) 05 57 51 33 63

Jacques Thienpoint

wine@thienpontwine.com

Pomerol

3 ha; 7,000 bottles

[map p. 30]

The pine tree that gave its name to the property still towers over it, although the old house has been replaced by a contemporary jewel of a winery. When Jacques Thienpont started Le Pin in 1979, he had no idea it was going to become one of the most famous—and at one time the most expensive—wines of Pomerol. The tiny vineyard of 1.2 ha is located between Vieux Château Certan (owned by the Thienpont family) and Trotanoy. The original plan was to add it to Vieux Château Certan, but the family did not want to pay the price, so Jacques bought it together with his uncle and his father, and became responsible for the winemaking. Later Jacques bought his uncle's and father's shares. In 1984 he added the adjacent plot. The team at Vieux Château Certan looks after the vines.

There's no second wine, but there is selection, and barrels that don't make it are relegated to generic Pomerol. Jacques also makes Trilogia, a blend of three vintages. Variety in terroir is shown by the range of individual barrels from rich and full (but tight) to super-smooth elegance. The blend belies the monovarietal composition by its refinement. Longevity is indicated by the fact that the 1998 was at a point of perfect balance between mature and primary influences in 2014. Intending to repeat his success, Jacques has bought Château Haut Plantey, a derelict property with good terroir on St Emilion's limestone plateau, renamed it as L'If, and plans to make it the Le Pin of St. Emilion.

Château Quintus ✶

 1 Larosé, 33300 St. Emilion

☎ (33) 05 57 24 69 44

François Capdemourlin

@ info@chateau-quintus.com

🌐 www.chateau-quintus.com

◉ St. Emilion

② Le Dragon de Quintus

🌱 28 ha; 76,000 bottles

[map p. 31]

Tertre Daugay was the fifth château to be bought by Clarence Dillon holdings (owners of Château Haut Brion), so they renamed it Quintus in 2011. Two years later they purchased neighboring Château l'Arrosée and merged it into Quintus, more or less doubling the size. (Quintus is not the fifth estate but the fifth great wine, says manager François Capdemourlin, who was previously at L'Arrosée.)

The combined estates occupy a small hill at the southwest corner of the limestone plateau. Tertre Daugay is higher up, and from it you can look down on L'Arrosée. At about 60m, this is the second highest elevation in the appellation, and you can see across to a panorama of grand cru classés in front of the church at St. Emilion.

Quintus usually comes from the top of the hill and the slopes, the second wine comes from the bottom of the hill, and a third wine (introduced in 2014 and labeled just as St. Emilion) comes from the plain below. But all lots are tasted blind to do the selection. Blending takes place before aging for 12 months. Quintus has 35-40% new oak, and the second wine has 25-30%. Quintus and the second wine are made at Tertre Daugay; the St. Emilion is made at L'Arrosée. Each has a dedicated team. There are plans to construct a new tasting room at Tertre Daugay.

Plantings are typical for St. Emilion, with 70% Merlot, 26% Cabernet Franc, and 4% Cabernet Sauvignon (some Cabernet Sauvignon has been removed). The second wine follows the style of the grand vin, but with less intensity. Vintage character shows clearly in both wines, with more acidity in 2014, richer and softer in 2015, but with the same relative difference between them. I find that the extra refinement of Quintus makes it seem more driven by Cabernet Franc, even though the blend is similar in both grand vin and second wine. "We want this to be a wine for pleasure, we want people to finish the bottle and open another. It should not be over-ripe or too oaky," François says.

Château Roc de Cambes **

ROC DE CAMBES

2005

CÔTES DE BOURG

François et Emilie Mitjavile

◎ 3 Au Roc, 33710 Bourg

📞 (33) 05 57 24 75 46

@ contact@roc.de.cambes.com

🌐 roc-de-cambes.com

◐ Côtes de Bourg

🕮 ⁄⁄

🍃 12 ha; 45,000 bottles

[map p. 28]

This is by far and away the most expensive wine of the Côtes de Bourg. When François Mitjavile purchased the property in 1987, it was dilapidated, but had good terroir and old vines. François is amused by the often-told story that he put his finger in the soil and decided to buy the property. "It is astonishing people should think I work like that."

Merlot is the driving force; the wines usually also have up to 20% Cabernet Sauvignon and 5% Malbec. "The terroir is homogeneous and there are few differences between the plots where Cabernet and Merlot are planted. There are difficulties with Cabernet Sauvignon because it ripens late. In dry years we get a superb maturity of Cabernet Sauvignon, we like the effect of having the Cabernet Sauvignon, but it's more a matter of the aromatic complexity it brings than the structure," says Nina Mitjavile. As at the Mitjavile's other property, Château Tertre Rôteboeuf in St. Emilion, all the efforts go into one wine.

When young, Roc de Cambes is more evidently forceful than Tertre Rôteboeuf, perhaps because the fruits in St. Emilion are so much richer as to hide the structure. But as the wines age, there seems to me to be something of a convergence in style, with Roc de Cambes becoming more like Tertre Rôteboeuf in its overall balance. "Proximity to the Gironde, and the presence of Cabernet Sauvignon, a Médocain aspect," says François The 2000 vintage of Roc de Cambes unusually had equal proportions of Cabernet and Merlot, and (showing well in 2013), remains my favorite.

Château Rol Valentin   *

 5, les Cabannes Sud, 33330 St. Emilion

 (33) 05 57 74 43 51

 Alexandra & Nicolas Robin

 contact@vignoblesrobin.com

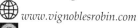 www.vignoblesrobin.com

 St. Emilion

 Les Valentines

8 ha; 40,000 bottles
[map p. 31]

Rol Valentin was established in 1994 by Eric Prissette, a soccer star, and sold to its present owners, Alexandra and Nicolas Robin, in 2009. (Alex is the daughter of supermarket Leclerc's chief wine buyer, and Nicolas is the nephew of the Robin sisters of Le Gay and Lafleur.) Vineyards are divided into two parts, one on sandy soils to the west, one on clay and limestone soils to the east. The small winery feels like an extended residence, in the middle of the plot of western vineyards, but there is a project to construct a new winery at the other site, built into a slope for gravity-feed operation. "It will be modern, but not too contemporary," says Alex Robin. The Robins also own Clos Vieux Taillefer in Pomerol (the vineyards were in the family), and Château de Laussac in Castillon. Stéphane Derenoncourt is the consulting winemaker.

Plantings have been 90% Merlot and 10% Cabernet Franc, but 5% Malbec has just been added near the house; the first year it's included in the wine is 2018. The grand vin has had something of a reputation as a garage wine, but in fact it's aged half in new oak, 40% in 1-year oak, and 10% in cuve to keep freshness. The latter is a big concern. "We harvest in the morning, and the grapes are in the vat by lunch time, we want to harvest as fresh as possible," Alex says. Lots are selected for the grand vin or second wine at the end of barrel-aging. The second wine is about 25% of production.

The second wine is easy and approachable. Rol Valentin has sometimes been called a garage wine, but in spite of its high content of Merlot, gives a good impression of the Cabernet Franc of St. Emilion. "For the second wine we look for something fruity and round, it should be ready to drink on release, and should last 5-7 years. Rol Valentin is more structured, it has more complexity, and should last longer," Alex says.

Some critics consider that Rol Valentin should have been promoted to grand cru classé. "We think on the basis of tasting we have the potential to be classified," Alex says. The new winery is intended as a step in that direction.

Château Le Tertre Rôteboeuf ★★★

TERTRE ROTEBOEUF

2005

SAINT-EMILION GRAND CRU

François et Emilie Mitjavile

○ 33330 Saint Laurent-des-Combes

☏ (33) 05 57 24 75 46

François Mitjavile

@ contact@tertre-roteboeuf.com

⊕ www.tertre-roteboeuf.com

◼ St. Emilion

📅❗ ◺

🍷 6 ha; 27,000 bottles

[map p. 31]

François Mitjavile marches to the beat of his own drum: a discussion with him at the château tends to take a philosophical direction, but always returns to issues of style and quality. Tertre Rôteboeuf is generally regarded as one of the top wines of St. Emilion, but it is not a Grand Cru Classé. "Classification is a very good thing but it is static. I had too much pride to apply and am very content to remain outside it," François explains.

The château produces only the grand vin: it is one of the few at this level to have no second wine. In fact, François does not believe in second wines. "With a homogeneous terroir, it is more interesting not to make a selection for a second wine, because production of a single wine best expresses the variations of the vintage, as the fruits ripen differently every year. A second wine is more suitable for properties which have heterogeneous terroirs," he says.

Pruning follows a cordon system as opposed to the Guyot that is common in St. Emilion, and there is no green harvesting. Picking is late to get full ripeness. The wine of Tertre Rôteboeuf is in the modern idiom, with full fruits matured in 100% new oak, but François does not see this as equivalent to powerful. "The wine is rich in flavor, but that does not mean powerful," he says. "This can be seen from the analysis of tannins." That said, I've always found Tertre Rôteboeuf to be an over-performer in lesser years, but definitely to need time to calm down in great years.

Château Troplong Mondot ✦✦

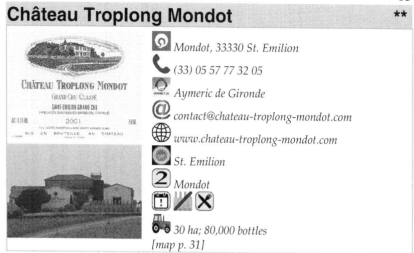

⊙ *Mondot, 33330 St. Emilion*

☎ *(33) 05 57 77 32 05*

✉ *Aymeric de Gironde*

@ *contact@chateau-troplong-mondot.com*

🌐 *www.chateau-troplong-mondot.com*

◉ *St. Emilion*

② *Mondot*

🚜 *30 ha; 80,000 bottles*

[map p. 31]

Situated on a high point (106 meters) on the limestone plateau a couple of miles to the east of the town of St. Emilion, Troplong Mondot has a view all the way across to the spire of the church in the town. The château preceded the vineyards and dates from the eighteenth century. The property was purchased by the Valette family, originally wine merchants from Paris, in 1936. Under Christine Valette, who inherited the property in 1981, the château expanded its activities with a guest house and a gourmet restaurant. Christine sadly died young in 2014, and the property was sold to a French insurance group, Scor, in 2017. (Purchase price was not revealed, but was rumored to be about 180 million.) Aymeric de Gironde, who was managing Château Cos d'Estournel in St. Estèphe, was appointed to manage the estate, which is now undergoing extensive renovation.

Essentially unchanged since they were created in the nineteenth century, vineyards are in a single block around the château, on a southwest-facing slope. They are planted with 90% Merlot; the rest is divided between Cabernet Franc and Cabernet Sauvignon. Average vine age is about 30 years. The soil is a mixture of clay and limestone. Advised by Michel Rolland, yields are low and the harvest is late, followed by traditional vinification, and élevage for 12-24 months in 75% new oak (the rest is one-year old oak).

From a middle of the road reputation, the wine improved to the point of promotion to Premier Grand Cru Classé in 2006. "Our wine is complex, tannic, difficult to drink when young," Christine Valette used to say. "It needs explanation and a certain knowledge." Indeed, the wine can show a tannic bite when young, although this is usually followed by soft black aromatics.

Château Trotanoy ***

Chemin de la Cabanne, 33500 Pomerol

(33) 05 57 51 78 96

Geneviève Sandifer

info@jpmoueix.com

www.moueix.com

Pomerol

Espérance de Trotanoy

7 ha; 25,000 bottles

[map p. 30]

A long avenue of trees leads to the modest château that is Trotanoy, but in Moueix's discrete fashion, there is no sign at the entrance. The property was bought by Jean-Pierre Moueix in 1953. It dates from the eighteenth century, when its name originated as a shortening of Trop Ennuie (referring to the difficulty of working the soils). This is a warm, gravelly area, protected enough that many of the vines survived the great freeze of 1956. Underneath the gravel, or the black clay of some parts, is the famous *casse de fer* (iron-rich subsoil). Average vine age today is about 40 years.

Trotanoy is usually the first of the Moueix estates to be harvested. The combination of old vines, microclimate, and terroir makes for a powerful wine. "Trotanoy is the most massive of the Moueix properties," says export manager Frédéric Lospied. Élevage lasts about 20 months in barriques with 50% new wood. Perhaps these days Trotanoy is a little more restrained, or rather a bit more precise, than it used to be. The wines of the sixties and seventies were splendid, with the 1961 showing dense black structure, and the 1970 and 1971 all opulence.

Recent vintages show good grip and underlying structure to balance the richness of the fruits, which are 90% Merlot. Christian Moueix might describe Trotanoy as the "poor man's Petrus," but the style is not the same, upright versus broad, gravel versus clay, even a little austere when young. A wine of real character, this is always one of the top Pomerols. Since 2009 a second wine, Espérance de Trotanoy, has been made in some years from parcels in the northeast part of the vineyard.

Château Trottevieille ★★

○ *Trottevieille, 33330 St. Emilion*

☎ *(33) 05 57 24 71 34*

○ *Philippe Casteja*

@ *domaines@borie-manoux.fr*

⊕ *www.trottevieille.com*

◉ *St. Emilion*

② *La Vieille Dame de Trottevieille*

🚶🔀

🚜 *10 ha; 36,000 bottles*

[map p. 31]

One of the oldest estates in Pomerol—the name refers to an old lady who lived there in the fifteenth century—Trottevieille claims to have some of the oldest vines in Bordeaux including Cabernet Franc surviving from before phylloxera. (A special cuvée from these vines was produced in 2004.) Trottevieille is one of several properties owned by the Castéja family (of the Borie-Manoux negociant), and recently they have been trying to improve the quality, which in the past has tended to be a little rustic.

At one time Trottevieille was the only Premier Grand Cru Classé to the east of St. Emilion. In a single block around the Château on the limestone plateau, the vineyards have red clay on top of the limestone. There's a substantial proportion of Cabernet Franc, usually a little over 40% in the grand vin, and also a small amount of Cabernet Sauvignon, so the wine is less dominated by Merlot than the average for St. Emilion. Vinification is standard: cold soak, fermentation, and maturation in new oak for up to 18 months. Major improvements have occurred since 2002, when the second wine was introduced (although it's usually only around 10% of production).

One of the other châteaux owned by Philippe Castéja is Batailley in Pauillac, and in spite of the evident differences between left bank and right bank, there seems to me to be a similar sturdy character in the styles of the two properties. These are solid wines, and can be good value, but I don't usually find them really exciting.

Château Valandraud ***

33330 Saint-Étienne-de-Lisse

(33) 05 57 55 09 13

Jean-Luc Thunevin

thunevin@thunevin.com

www.thunevin.com

St. Emilion

Virginie de Valandraud

9 ha; 35,000 bottles
[map p. 32]

Valandraud embodies St. Emilion's development over the past twenty years. Jean-Luc Thunevin came from Algeria, opened a wine shop, became a negociant, and began buying land. From his first plot of 0.6 ha (near Pavie Macquin) he made the first vintage of Valandraud in 1991 in the garage adjacent to his house, only 1,200 bottles. (Valandraud is a play on his wife's maiden name.)

Everything was done by hand, from deleafing in the vineyard to destemming before vinification. "I was the first garagiste. We protected the fruits, took precautions against oxidation, introduced green harvest, leaf pulling. Everyone does it now," Jean-Luc says. The defining year was 1995, when 200% new oak was used (racking from new oak into new oak). The wine made a great reputation, achieving a price to match the first growths, although its super-extraction and oakiness were controversial. Ageability was questioned. "Happily we can now make wines that are good now and age well. When I started people said Valandraud would not last more than ten years, but now it has lasted thirty years," Jean-Luc points out.

The original terroir was undistinguished, but subsequent purchases have built up more extensive vineyards in the area of St. Etienne to the east, and now there is even a real château. The movement has been validated, or come full circle, with the inclusion of Valandraud as a Premier Grand Cru Classé in 2012. Today it's just 100% new oak, and the style is less flamboyant. By 2015 it was quite elegant, admittedly modern in style, but no longer the outrageous garage wine.

Vieux Château Certan ★★

Vieux Château Certan
Grand Vin
POMEROL
2006

Appellation Pomerol controlée
SOCIÉTÉ CIVILE DU VIEUX CHÂTEAU CERTAN
PROPRIÉTAIRE À POMEROL (FRANCE)
MIS EN BOUTEILLE AU CHÂTEAU

📍 *1, Route de Lussac (D121), 33500 Pomerol*

📞 *(33) 05 57 51 17 33*

👤 *Alexandre Thienpoint*

@ *info@vieuxchateaucertan.com*

🌐 *www.vieuxchateaucertan.com*

⬤ *Pomerol*

② *La Gravette de Certan*

🏭

🍷 *14 ha; 50,000 bottles*
[map p. 30]

One of the oldest properties in Pomerol, Vieux Château Certan has been held by the Thienpont family since 1924, and they are proud of its history. "It's exactly the same as it was in 1745," says Alexandre Thienpont, who has been running the property since 1985. Vineyards are in a single block around the château, some on buttonhole clay similar to adjacent Petrus. They are divided into 23 plots that are vinified separately. Plantings are 60% Merlot, 30% Cabernet Franc, and 10% Cabernet Sauvignon, with Merlot on clay, and the Cabernets on areas of gravel. Unusual for Pomerol, the high proportion of Cabernet gives Vieux Château Certan a distinctive restraint, with a balance in the direction of St. Emilion.

Fermentation in wooden vats is followed by élevage for 18-22 months. "Because alcohol is getting higher now, new oak was reduced from 100% in 2008, to 80% in 2009 and 2010, to 67% today," Alexandre explains. Alexandre's son Guillaume has been involved since 2011 and the style is changing further as a result: "It is more focused on concentration (as opposed to power) and he would regard the wine we are tasting (the 2006) as old fashioned." So picking is now a little bit later, there is a saignée, and there is a touch more pump-over. Vieux Château Certan can be a relative bargain: because ownership is spread among 44 members of the Thienpont family, there is a constant need for cash flow to generate dividends, so the wine is always priced to sell quickly.

Mini-Profiles of Important Estates

Château Ampélia

Bouzy, 33330 Saint Philippe d'Aiguille
(33) 05 57 25 19 94
François Despagne
contact@grand-corbin-despagne.com
www.grand-corbin-despagne.com/en/chateau-ampelia-en

② *La Dame d'Ampélia*

5 ha; 25,000 bottles
[map p. 32]

After inheriting Château Corbin-Despagne in 1996 (see mini-profile), three years later François Despagne decided in addition to create a new domain in the Côtes de Castillon. Located at the highest point in the appellation (110m), the vineyard is planted 95% with Merlot, 5% with Cabernet Franc. The first vintage was 2000. A new cellar was constructed in 2004. The wine is aged in new, 2-year, and 3-year barriques.

Château Balestard la Tonnelle

33330 St. Emilion
(33) 05 57 74 02 06
Thierry Capdemourlin
info@vignoblescapdemourlin.com
vignobles-capdemourlin.fr

② *Chanoine de Balestard*

12 ha; 60,000 bottles
[map p. 31]

This old estate originated in the fifteenth century, and is named for Canon Balestard and the tower (La Tonnelle) on the property, which has become its symbol. A grand cru classé, it has been in the Capdemourlin family since 1923; they also own Cap de Mourlin nearby, and Château Roudier in Montagne St. Emilion. They sold Petit Faurie de Soutard in 2017. Plantings are 70% Merlot, 25% Cabernet Franc, and 5% Cabernet Sauvignon. The wine is aged in an equal mix of new oak and 1-year barriques. A sturdy wine, it is best enjoyed on the younger side. Michel Rolland is the consulting winemaker.

Château Barde-Haut

33330 Saint-Christophe-des-Bardes
(33) 05 57 25 72 55
Hélène Garcin-Levêque
info@vignoblesgarcin.com
www.chateaubardehaut.com

② *Le Vallon de Barde-Haut*

17 ha; 60,000 bottles
[map p. 31]

Located at the far east of St. Emilion, the château was purchased in 2000 by Sylviane Garcin-Cathiard, who owns Clos l'Église in Pomerol (see mini-profile), and Haut-Bergey and Château Branon in Léognan. A new chai was built in 2002, and the buildings were renovated in 2012. The estate is managed by her daughter Hélène and son-in-law Patrice Lévêque, and was promoted to grand cru classé in 2012. Merlot-driven (85%), the wine is aged entirely in new oak.

Château Bellevue Mondotte

33330 St. Emilion
(33) 05 57 55 43 43
Henrique da Costa
vignobles.perse@wanadoo.fr
www.vignoblesperse.com

3 ha; 4,800 bottles

This is a super-cuvée coming from a plot that Gérard Perse purchased in 2001; it's an enclave within Château Pavie-Decesse (see mini-profile) on the limestone plateau. Merlot is 90%, with 5% each of Cabernet Sauvignon and Cabernet Franc; vines average 45-years-old. Yields are kept very low in the style of garage wines. Aged in 100% new oak, the wine is made by the team at Château Pavie with Michel Rolland as consultant.

Château Bonalgue

24 Rue Bonalgue, 33500 Libourne
(33) 05 57 51 62 17
Nadège Sabras
jbbourotte@jbaudy.fr
www.jbaudy.fr/#/bonalgue

 Beauséjour de Bonalgue

10 ha; 35,000 bottles
[map p. 30]

The Audy family have been negociants in Libourne since the start of the twentieth century. Along the way, they acquired several châteaux, including Bonalgue in Pomerol in 1926. Pierre Bourotte, grandson of the founder, took over in 1969, and in 2003 his son, Jean-Baptiste, took over. The property is located close to the town of Libourne at the northeast; vineyards are 90% Merlot. The wine is aged in half new, half one-year barriques, and has a good reputation, although the château is not on the famous plateau with the best terroir.

Château Chauvin

1, Les Cabanes-Nord, 33330 St. Emilion
(33) 05 57 24 76 25
Sylvie Cazes
chateauchauvingcc@wanadoo.fr
www.chateauchauvin.com

 *Folie de Chauvin*

15 ha; 55,000 bottles
[map p. 31]

This was once part of the large Corbin estate, in the northwest part of St. Emilion near Pomerol, and was created when Corbin was divided in 1852. It was purchased by the Ondet family in 1891, and became a grand cru classé in 1955. Then in 2014 it was purchased by Sylvie Cazes, formerly of Château Pichon Lalande in Pauillac; Philippe Moureau came from Pichon Lalande to run the estate, which is planted with 75% Merlot. As of the 2015 vintage, I have not seen any change in the light, elegant style. I would place the wine at the level of a good Cru Bourgeois from the Médoc. The second wine was La Borderie de Chauvin but has been renamed as Folie de Chauvin.

Clos de L'Oratoire

33330 St. Emilion
(33) 05 57 24 71 33
Stephan von Neipperg
info@neipperg.com
www.neipperg.com

 13 ha; 45,000 bottles

Vignobles Neipperg, which owns premier grand cru classé Château Canon La Gaffelière, bought this property in 1972, located in the northeast corner of the appellation. Clos de l'Oratoire originated when the best lots were split off from Château Peyreau in the 1960s (also owned by Neipperg). It became a grand cru classé in 1969; by comparison with Canon La Gaffelière (see profile), which is equivalent to a classified growth in the Médoc, it shows a refreshing, lighter, style, equivalent to a Cru Bourgeois. Plantings are 80% Merlot; there is 50-70% new oak for aging.

Clos des Jacobins

4 Gomerie, 33330 St. Emilion
(33) 05 57 51 19 91
Magali & Thibaut Decoster
contact@mtdecoster.
www.mtdecoster.com

 *Prieur des Jacobins*

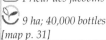 *9 ha; 40,000 bottles*
[map p. 31]

Clos des Jacobins was bought by the Cordier negociant family in 1964, then when Cordier sold off most of their properties, passed rapidly into the hands of Marionnaud in 2001 and on to the Decoster family in 2004. The Decosters also own Châteaux La Commanderie and Candale in St. Emilion. Another branch of the family owns Château Fleur Cardinale. The estate is in two parts: the château and main vineyard are close to the village of St. Emilion; there is also another parcel near Angélus. Vineyards are planted with 80% Merlot. The wine is aged in 80% new barriques. Hubert de Boüard has been the consulting winemaker since 2001; accordingly the style tends to be rich and fruity.

Clos L'Église

33500 Pomerol
(33) 05 56 64 05 22
Hélène Garcin-Levêque
info@vignoblesgarcin.com
www.vignoblesgarcin.com

 Esprit de l'Eglise

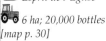 *6 ha; 20,000 bottles*
[map p. 30]

This is the jewel in the crown of Vignobles Garcin, the first property that Sylviane Garcin-Cathiard purchased on the right bank, in 1997. Château Barde Haut (see mini-profile) was purchased later. She also owns châteaux in Pessac-Léognan. In the eighteenth century, Clos l'Église was twice its present size, but then half was split off to form L'Église-Clinet. (Neither is to be confused with Domaine l'Église.) The vineyards are on the famous crasse de fer terroir. Hélène Garcin et Patrice Lévêque have been in charge since the acquisition. They modernized the cellars and the wine has been steadily improving. The approach is unconventional. Against the modern trend of picking everything at uniform ripeness, they are both the first and last to pick in Pomerol. "All of the fruit is picked ripe, of course, but there are differences such as how chewy the fruit is, whether the seeds are ripe or not, this is all based on feelings in the mouth and common sense," says Hélène. She believes that uniform ripeness loses complexity in the wine. "By starting the harvest early and finishing late we get a much wider range of ripeness, which is not how it used to be, but what we gain is complexity and elegance." Based on 70% Merlot, with an average vine age of 35 years, the wine is aged entirely in new barriques. The second wine is Esprit de l'Église.

Clos Puy Arnaud

7 Puy Arnaud, 33350 Belvès
de Castillon
(33) 05 57 47 90 33
Thierry Valette
clospuyarnaud@wanadoo.fr
clospuyarnaud.com

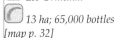 *Les Ormeaux*

 13 ha; 65,000 bottles
[map p. 32]

The Valette family has long been involved with wine, owning a negociant and several châteaux that at one time included Pavie and Troplong-Mondot. In 2000, Thierry Valette purchased Clos Puy Arnaud: before the classification of St. Emilion in 1955, it was considered part of that appellation, but since then has been Côtes de Castillon. Most of the terroir is similar to the *calcaire à astéries* of the St. Emilion limestone plateau. Plantings are 70% Merlot today, but the plan is to increase Cabernet Franc to 40%. New oak is about 25% for the grand vin. Since 2014 there has been a second wine, Les Ormeaux. In addition, there are two lighter wines, Cuvée Pervenche and Cuvée Bistrot (for immediate enjoyment).

Château La Clotte

1 rue Bergat, 33330 St. Emilion
(33) 05 57 24 24 57
Pauline Vauthier
fax; (33) 05 57 24 79 67

4 ha; 10,000 bottles
[map p. 31]

The tiny vineyard is located just outside the village, and the cuverie is inside. It was purchased by the Chailleau family at the start of the twentieth century. At the end of the century, it was managed by Moueix, but Nelly Mouilerac (Sylvain Chailleau's granddaughter) took over in 1999 when the contract with Moueix expired. A majority share in the estate was sold to Alain Vauthier of Château Ausone in 2014. The vineyard is planted with 80% Merlot. La Clotte has generally been felt to have under-performed, but has gained a new reputation since the sale. There is no longer a second wine, yields have been reduced, and new oak increased to 85%.

Château La Couspaude

33330 St. Emilion
(33) 05 57 40 15 76
Yohan Aubert
vignobles.aubert@wanadoo.fr
www.aubert-vignobles.com

7 ha; 36,000 bottles
[map p. 31]

Close to the village, this is the star in the Aubert family's portfolio of eight châteaux, which came into the family by marriage in 1963. The Auberts restored the property, which became a grand cru classé in 1996. It has a classic makeup in the vineyards: 70% Merlot, 20% Cabernet Franc, and 5% Cabernet Sauvignon. The wine is often felt to reflect the mark of Michel Rolland, the consulting winemaker, in a powerful rich style enhanced by use of 100% new oak.

Château La Croix de Gay

8 Route de Saint-Jacques-de-Compostelle, 33500 Pomerol
(33) 05 57 51 19 05
Chantal Lebreton
contact@chateau-lacroixdegay.com
www.chateau-lacroixdegay.com

5 ha; 25,000 bottles
[map p. 30]

This old estate has long been in the same family, but has a history of ups and downs. It expanded in the 1960s when it was managed by Noel Raynaud. His son Alain and daughter Chantal Lebreton took over in 1998. Then in 2012, Croix de Gay sold 15 ha of its vineyards to Château l'Évangile, greatly reducing the size of the estate. Alain Raynaud left, and has become one of Bordeaux's best-known consulting oenologists; Chantal continues to run the estate. A new cellar was built in 2014. The estate has 10 parcels, planted with 95% Merlot. Croix de Gay is aged in 50% new oak and 50% 1-year barriques. The top wine is Château La Fleur de Gay; made since 1982, from 2 ha of three parcels of the oldest vines, it ages in 100% new oak and accounts for about a quarter of production.

Château Faugères

33330 St-Étienne-de-Lisse
(33) 05 57 40 34 99
Yann Buchwalter
info@chateau-faugeres.com
www.chateau-faugeres.com

The estate extends from the far east of the St. Emilion appellation into the Côtes de Castillon, and makes three wines: Château Faugères and Château Péby-Faugères (both promoted to grand cru classé in St. Emilion in 2012), and Cap de Faugères (from the vineyards in Côtes de Castillon). The estate had been languishing, and began to revive in 1987 when it was inherited by Pierre-Bernard Guisez, but following its purchase in 2005 by Silvio Denz (of Lalique), there has been great investment in the

37 ha; 110,000 bottles
[map p. 32]

vineyards, and a modernistic cuverie—they call it a chai-cathedral—was constructed in 2009. Plantings are 85% Merlot, including an 8 ha plot of very old vines that has made the monovarietal Péby-Faugères since 1998. The wines age in half new and half one-year barriques.

Château Feytit Clinet

1 Feytit, 33500 Pomerol
(33) 05 57 25 51 27
Jeremy Chasseuil
jeremy.chasseuil@orange.fr

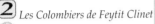

 Les Colombiers de Feytit Clinet

 7 ha; 35,000 bottles
[map p. 30]

A property belonging to the Chasseuil family, Château Feytit Client was managed by Moueix until Jeremy Chasseuil took over in 2000. This is a classic Pomerol estate, on the central plateau, with Merlot occupying 90% of the vineyards. There is nothing fancy about the facilities, but by reducing yields and modernizing production (increasing new oak to 75%), Jeremy has renovated the property. It's generally felt to have been on a roll for the past few years.

Château Fleur Cardinale

1 Petit Bois, 33330 St Étienne de Lisse
(33) 05 57 40 14 05
Florence & Dominique Decoster
contact@fleurcardinale.com
www.fleurcardinale.com

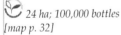 Bois Cardinale

 24 ha; 100,000 bottles
[map p. 32]

Having sold their porcelain business in Limoges, Florence and Dominique Decoster bought Fleur Cardinale in 2001. Located at the far east of St. Emilion, close to the border with Castillon, the estate was enlarged by 4 ha by including part of La Croix Cardinale (purchased in 2011), after the addition was approved when Fleur Cardinale was promoted to grand cru classé in 2012. The other half of Croix Cardinale continues to be produced as a separate wine. Jean-Luc Thunevin, of nearby Château Valandraud, is the consulting winemaker. Not surprisingly, the Fleur Cardinale is aged in 100% new barriques, and tends to richness and power. The second wine, Bois Cardinale, comes mostly from younger vines, and is aged in 70% new oak. Until 2012, Secret de Cardinale was a small production run from a 1 ha plot adjacent to Fleur Cardinale.

Château Fonroque

Fonroque, 33330 St. Emilion
(33) 05 57 24 60 02
Alain Moueix
info@chateaufonroque.com
www.chateaufonroque.net

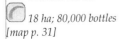 Château Cartier

18 ha; 80,000 bottles
[map p. 31]

Fonroque was the first property the Moueix family bought in St. Emilion, in 1931. It's been a grand cru classé since 1955. Alain Moueix, who owned it with the Curats, his aunt and uncle, was in charge from 2001 until it was sold in 2017 to the Guillard family, owners of an insurance group. Alain has stayed on as a consultant. Located on the limestone plateau, in a single block, it is planted with 80% Merlot. The grand vin is aged in 30% new oak. The second wine is aged party in old barriques and partly in cuve, and is about a third of production. The new owners plan to renovate the estate; it remains to be seen whether the style will change.

Château Franc Mayne

RD 243, 14 La Gomerie, 33330 St. Emilion
(33) 05 57 24 62 61
Martine Cazeneuve
info@chateaufrancmayne.com
www.chateaufrancmayne.com

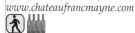

 *Les Cèdres de Franc-Mayne*

 7 ha; 30,000 bottles
[map p. 31]

Located just to the northwest of the village, this grand cru classé has had various owners recently, AXA from 1984 to 1996, then a Belgian negociant, Fourcroy, and since 2005 the Laviale family, who own Châteaux Lussac and Vieux Maillet. The Laviales have constructed a new cuverie (with impressive underground facilities in the old caves) and added accommodation (the Relais Franc Mayne) with a splendid view over the vineyards. The Laviales introduced 10% Cabernet Franc, so the grand vin is 90% Merlot; it's aged in almost all new oak. The second wine comes from younger vines and is Merlot. Michel Rolland consults.

Gracia

1136 Rue du Thau, 33330 St. Emilion
(33) 05 57 24 77 98
Michel Gracia
michelgracia@wanadoo.fr

 Les Angelots de Gracia

 3 ha; 8,000 bottles
[map p. 31]

A garage wine, created in 1997 by stonemason Michel Gracia from a tiny plot of 1.34 ha near Château Troplong-Mondot, Gracia continues to hold its reputation. Holdings have been expanded, with some parcels near Angélus, and with 80% Merlot, 15% Cabernet Franc, and 5% Cabernet Sauvignon offers more variety than the monovarietal Merlot that's typical of garage wines. The wine is aged, of course, in 100% new oak. Les Angelots comes from a plot of 1.25 ha near Angélus, and is a separate cuvée (produced since 2007) more than a second wine.

Château Grand Corbin

5 Grand Corbin, 33330 St. Emilion
(33) 05 57 24 70 62
Philippe Dambrine
contact@grand-corbin.com
www.grand-corbin.com

 Château Tour du Pin Franc

29 ha; 150,000 bottles
[map p. 31]

Owned by the SMABTP insurance group, this is a fusion between the 6 ha Château Haut Corbin (purchased in 1986) and adjacent 15 ha Château Grand Corbin (purchased in 2010 from the Giraud family). Grand Corbin was in the 1955 classification, demoted in 1996, and reinstated in 2006. The combined château was included in 2012. Since the merger, the estate has expanded by another 7 ha of adjacent vineyards. Plantings are 75% Merlot, 25% Cabernet Franc, and 5% Cabernet Sauvignon; average age of the vines is 40 years. SMABTP also owns Château Cantemerle in the Médoc. Philippe Dambrine is the winemaker at both.

Château Grand Mayne

1 Le Grand Mayne, 33330 St. Emilion
(33) 05 57 74 42 50
Jean-Antoine Nony
grand-mayne@grand-mayne.com
www.chateau-grand-mayne.com

Grand Mayne is one of the right bank properties actually housed in a château, or perhaps more of a grand manor house. The estate at one time was much larger, but most was sold off. Its modern era began in 1934, when Bordeaux negociant Jean Nony purchased the estate. His grandsons run it today. It has been a grand cru classé since 1955. The vineyard is in a single block at the west, at the foot of the plateau; the part on the slopes has limestone;

94

Filia de Grand Mayne

 17 ha; 60,000 bottles [map p. 31]

at the base, the soil is more sandy. The grand vin is typically 75% Merlot, 20% Cabernet Franc, 5% Cabernet Sauvignon; the second wine comes from young (less than 20-year) vines, and has a fraction more Merlot. Both are aged in 70% new oak.

Château Grand Pontet

1 Les Trois Moulins, 33330 St. Emilion
(33) 05 57 74 46 88
Sylvie Pourquet-Bécot
chateau.grand-pontet@wanadoo.fr
www.chateaugrandpontet.com

 Dauphin de Grand Pontet

 14 ha; 70,000 bottles [map p. 31]

Located adjacent to Château Beauséjour-Bécot, the property was purchased by Gerard and Dominique Bécot of Beauséjour-Bécot in 1980 from the negociant Barton & Guestier. It is managed by Sylvia Pourquet-Bécot, Gerard's sister. Vineyards are in a single block. The soils at Grand Pontet have more clay, so the wine has more solidity: it's sometimes described as old-school. Plantings are 70% Merlot with 15% each of Cabernet Franc and Cabernet Sauvignon; the wine is aged in about three quarters new oak. The second wine comes from younger vines but is not made in every vintage.

Château La Grave à Pomerol

Jean-Pierre Moueix, 54, Quai du Priourat, BP 129, 33500 Libourne
(33) 05 57 51 78 96
Geneviève Sandifer
info@jpmoueix.com
www.moueix.com/en/pomerol/lagrave

 Domaine Trigant de Boisset

 9 ha; 36,000 bottles [map p. 30]

Christian Moueix purchased La Grave à Pomerol in 1971. As the name indicates, it is on gravelly soils, on the western slope of the Pomerol plateau. However, during the 1980s some of the more gravelly parcels were exchanged with some sandier parcels from La Fleur Petrus. The property is in the second tier of Moueix estates. Plantings are typical for Pomerol, with 85% Merlot and 15% Cabernet Sauvignon. It's aged in 40% new oak. Unusually for Moueix, there is a second wine, coming from younger vines, named Trigant de Boisset for the previous owners of the estate.

Château Gros Moulin

7 Lieu Dit Gros Moulin, 33710 Bourg-sur-Gironde
(33) 06 88 02 78 88
Rémy Eymas
chateau.gros.moulin@wanadoo.fr
www.chateaugrosmoulin.com

34 ha; 50,000 bottles [map p. 28]

The domain has been in the same family since 1757. Jacques Eymas handed over to his son Rémy in 2010. Just above Bourg, the estate is close to the Gironde. The range of wines is unusually wide for Bordeaux. Château Gros Moulin is the classic Côtes de Bourg blend dominated by Merlot. Also a Côtes de Bourg, Château Croûte-Mallard is essentially Malbec (there is 5% Merlot). They age in 1-, 2-, and 3-year barriques. There are two prestige cuvées: Per Vitem Ad Vitem is a Bourg with 60% Cabernet Franc and 20% each of Merlot and Malbec; Heritage 1757 is 60% Malbec and 40% Merlot. They see new oak, 60% for the first, 100% for the second. There's also a rosé, and a white from 0.5 ha of Sauvignon Blanc (Les Lys du Moulin Rosé and Les Lys du Moulin Blanc).

Château Guadet

4 rue Guadet, 33330 St. Emilion
(33) 05 57 74 40 04
Guy-Petrus or Vincent Lignac
chateauguadet@orange.fr
www.chateau-guadet-
saintemilion.fr

 *Le Jardin de Guadet*

6 ha; 24,000 bottles
[map p. 31]

The Guadets were an important family from the fifteenth century to the French Revolution. The vineyards are just outside the walls of St. Emilion, but the cuverie is actually inside the village. The property was known as Guadet-St. Julien until the name was simplified in 2004. A grand cru classé, it was demoted in 2006 and reinstated in 2012. The Lignac family bought the château in 1844: Vincent Lignac returned from winemaking in the New World to take over in 2010. Plantings are 75% Merlot; the wine is aged in 50% new oak. Even though the property is tiny, there is a second wine.

Château La Croix Taillefer

56 Route de Périgueux, 33500
Pomerol
05 57 25 08 65
Claude Rivière
la.croix.taillefer@wanadoo.fr

 6 ha
[map p. 30]

This was originally Château La Loubière, in what is probably one of the oldest winegrowing locations in Bordeaux. The Rivières bought a hectare of old Merlot vines here in 1997, and slowly added more plots to bring the domain to its present size. The terroir is black sand on top of *crasse de fer*. Plantings are 98% Merlot. The wine ages in new oak.

Château La Marzelle

La Marzelle, 33330 St. Emilion
(33) 05 57 55 10 55
Philippe Genevey
info@lamarzelle.com
www.lamarzelle.com

 *Prieuré La Marzelle*

17 ha; 60,000 bottles
[map p. 31]

The chais for La Marzelle stand just beyond the chais of the hotel Grand Barrail. Originally this was all one vineyard, but Grand Barrail was separated in 1956. la Marzelle was purchased in 1997 by Jean Jacques and Jacqueline Sioen, who have been rebuilding the estate. La Marzelle was declassified in the contested St. Emilion reclassification in 2006, and restored as a grand cru classé in 2012. Vineyards are planted with 75% Merlot, 17% Cabernet Franc, and 8% Cabernet Sauvignon. A small part of the crop is vinified in jars instead of in wood. The wine is moving in a modernist, not to say hedonistic, direction.

Château Lafleur-Gazin

33500 Pomerol
(33) 05 57 51 78 96
Geneviève Sandifer
info@jpmoueix.com
www.moueix.com/en/pomerol/lafleur-
gazin

9 ha; 40,000 bottles
[map p. 30]

Lafleur-Gazin has been owned by the Borderie family since 1930, but has been rented to Moueix since 1976. On the north edge of the Pomerol plateau, it's regarded as a bit of an under-achiever; Moueix describe it as "a lighter style of Pomerol." Vineyards are planted with a typical mix for Pomerol, with 85% Merlot. Barriques are about one third new oak for aging. Following Moueix's general policy, there is no second wine.

Domaine Léandre-Chevalier

40 Route de l'Estuaire, 33390 Ang-lade
(33) 05 57 64 46 54 / 33 6 10 80 06 44
Dominique Léandre
contact@lhommecheval.com
www.lhommecheval.com

 3 ha
[map p. 28]

To say this domain is iconoclastic is something of an understatement. Located in the north of Bordeaux AOP, it's directly across the Gironde from Pauillac. Dominique took over the family domain in 1985, rejected mechanization, and decided "to return to the work of an artisan vigneron. My philosophy in wine is inspired more by Burgundy than Bordeaux." He started by reducing the size of the domain. He replanted the vineyards, some at extremely high density. Among them is a plot of Petit Verdot, derived from pre-phylloxera vines, and planted on its own roots. This is the 100% ProVocateur cuvée. Under Blaye Côtes de Bordeaux he has three wines: Le Queyroux is equal Merlot and Cabernet Sauvignon; Les Soeurettes and le Joyau also include a little Petit Verdot. Not surprisingly for an iconoclast, most of his cuvées are Vin de France, the most original being a two-pack of 11111 and 33333, both 100% Merlot, the difference being density of plantation (11,111 vines/ha versus 33,333 vines/ha).

Château Mazeyres

56 Avenue Georges Pompidou, 33500 Libourne
(33) 05 57 51 00 48
Stéphany Lesaînt
communication@mazeyres.com
www.mazeyres.com

 *Le Seuil de Mazeyres*

26 ha; 100,000 bottles
[map p. 30]

Located on the outskirts of Libourne, this is an old Pomerol domain, as witnessed by Roman ruins on the property. In the middle ages, it was a convent. It was purchased by an insurance group in 1988, and has been managed by Alain Moueix since 1992. Plantings are almost 75% Merlot, and there is a tiny amount of Petit Verdot (unusual for the right bank). The grand vin is aged 30% in new barriques, 50% in older barriques, and 20% in cuve: the second wine is aged half in barriques and half in cuve.

Château Monbousquet

33330 Saint-Sulpice-de-Faleyrens
(33) 05 57 24 67 19
Gérard Perse
contact@chateaumonbousquet.com
www.chateaumonbousquet.com

Angélique de Monbousquet

31 ha; 90,000 bottles
[map p. 31]

The first château that Gérard Perse acquired in Bordeaux, in 1993, Monbousquet served as something of a prototype for his later purchases of Pavie and others. Vineyards were replanted, drainage installed, and the cellars renovated. Away from the top terroirs of the limestone plateau, the terroir is a mix of sand, gravel, and calcareous soil. Monbousquet was promoted to grand cru classé in 2006. Cabernet Franc was increased, making the vineyards 60% Merlot, 30% Cabernet Franc, and 10% Cabernet Sauvignon. New oak is 60% for the grand vin. In addition to the grand vin and second wine, Monbousquet also produces one of the few white wines to come from within St. Emilion (labeled as Bordeaux). A share in the estate was sold to a pension fund in 2013 for tax reasons, but management remains unchanged.

Château Mondésir-Gazin

77 Route de l'Estuaire, 33390 Plas-sac
(33) 05 57 42 29 80
Marc Pasquet
mondesirgazin@gmail.com
www.mondesir-gazin.com

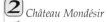 *Château Mondésir*

14 ha; 76,000 bottles
[map p. 28]

Formerly a photographer, Marc Pasquet and his wife Lawrence purchased this property in 1990. Situated close to the order between Blaye and Bourg, it has 9 ha in Blaye and 2 ha in Côtes de Bourg. Château Mondésir-Gazin comes from Blaye: Haut Mondésir comes from Côtes de Bourg. Merlot is the dominant variety in both, 70-80%% in Blaye, higher at 90% in Bourg. An unusual feature is that the second variety is Malbec for both. They age for 22 months in barriques with a quarter to a third new oak. The second wine, Château Mondésir, comes from Blaye, is 100% Merlot, and ages in cuve. There's also a St. Emilion, Château Gontey, from a 4 ha plot. Grapes have been planted to produce a white wine from 2018.

Château Montviel

1 Rue Grand Moulinet, 33500 Pomerol
(33) 05 57 25 34 34
Henri Parent
communication@montviel.com
www.vignoblespereverge.com

 La Rose Montviel

10 ha; 21,000 bottles
[map p. 30]

This was the first property acquired (in 1985) by Catherine Péré Vergé, who later bought Châteaux La Violette and La Gay (see profile), also in Pomerol. After her death in 2013, her son Henri Parent took over the management of the estates. A merger of three former properties, Montviel has two distinct terroirs, gravel with clay close to Clinet, and fine gravel with sand near Grand Moulinet. The overall size of the vineyards is 10 ha, divided into 27 plots, but only half are used to produce Château Montviel. La Rose Montviel comes from the other half. Plantings are 80% Merlot; Montviel ages in 100% new oak. Michel Rolland has been the consultant almost since the beginning (since 1988).

Château Pavie-Decesse

Lieu-dit Pavie Nord, 33330 St. Emilion
(33) 05 57 55 43 43
Gérard Perse
contact@vignoblesperse.com
www.chateaupavie.com

3 ha; 8,000 bottles
[map p. 31]

Gérard Perse bought Pavie-Decesse in 1997, a year before he bought Pavie (see profile), located just below. Pavie-Decesse was much reduced in size in 2002 by transferring 6 ha of vineyards on the slopes to Pavie: now Pavie-Decesse is a small vineyard confined to the plateau above. Facilities have been modernized and the wine is made in the same intense style as Pavie. Plantings are 90% Merlot (a much higher proportion than Pavie, which has only 60%). The vines are about 50 years old. Needless to say, it ages in 100% new oak. Michel Rolland is the consultant for all Perse properties.

Château la Pointe

18 Chemin de Gardelle, 33500 Libourne
(33) 05 57 51 02 11
Eric Monneret
contact@chateaulapointe.com
www.chateaulapointe.com

One of the the largest properties in Pomerol, this has been felt for some time to under-perform, although it was listed in the top group in the nineteenth century. It was owned by the d'Arfeuille family from 1941 until 2007, when it was sold to the insurance company Generali France. A new team was put in place to restore quality, Hubert de Boüard of Château Angélus was appointed as consulting oenologist. The project started with a soil

Pomerol de La Pointe

23 ha; 140,000 bottles

[map p. 30]

map of the vineyards, installing a drainage system and pulling out Cabernet Sauvignon so that plantings are now 85% Merlot and 15% Cabernet Franc. The cellars were renovated with smaller tanks to allow plot-by-plot vinification. The grand vin is now aged in 100% new oak instead of 50% new oak.

Château Rouget

6 Route de Saint Jacques de Compostelle, 33500 Pomerol
(33) 05 57 51 05 85
Edouard Labruyère
chateau.rouget@wanadoo.fr
www.chateau-rouget.com

 *Le Carillon de Rouget*

19 ha; 80,000 bottles

[map p. 30]

Located on the plateau of Pomerol near several famous château, Rouget occupies a site where winemaking is claimed to go back to Roman times. At the start of the twentieth century it was regarded as one of the more important châteaux, but its reputation declined, and much of the production was sold off to Moueix, until its purchase in 1992 by the Labruyère family, who also own Jacques Prieur in Meursault and properties in Beaujolais and Champagne. The cellars were renovated in 2001. Typical for the plateau, plantings are 85% Merlot. Part of the crop is vinified in barrique, the rest in vats. 50% new oak is used in aging. Michel Rolland is the consultant.

Château Simard

3 Simard, 33330 St. Emilion
(33) 05 57 24 24 57
Alain Vauthier
chateau.ausone@wanadoo.fr

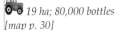

40 ha; 160,000 bottles

[map p. 31]

This large property in the south of the appellation was divided in two when the railway was built through it in 1870. It was purchased by the Mazière family in the 1920s, and came by inheritance in 2008 to Alain Vauthier of Château Ausone. Château Simard comes from the major part of the property. A smaller part of 8 ha, planted with 80% Merlot, makes Château Haut Simard. There is no named second wine, but there is a St. Emilion that comes from declassified lots.

Château Soutard

1 Soutard, 33330 St. Emilion
(33) 05 57 24 71 41
contact@soutard.com
www.chateau-soutard.com

 Les Jardins de Soutard

 30 ha; 100,000 bottles

[map p. 31]

The château is very grand for the right bank, built in 1471, and approached along a classic *allée* lined with trees. It remained in the hands of the same family for a century, until it was sold in 2006 to the insurance group La Mondiale, who already owned other châteaux in St. Emilion, Larmande, Grand Faurie La Rose, and Cadet-Piola. The château and its cellars were renovated. A grand cru classé since the start of the classification, Soutard was expanded (and improved) by adding the 7 ha of Cadet-Piola after approval by the reclassification of 2012. Plantings are 63% Merlot; the wine is aged in 60% new oak. The management is committed to oenotourism, with accommodation on site, and facilities for conferences.

Château Taillefer

30 Chemin de Taillefer, 33500 Libourne
(33) 05 57 25 50 45
Claire Moueix
contact@moueixbernard.com
www.moueixbernard.com

 Château Fontmarty

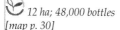 12 ha; 48,000 bottles
[map p. 30]

This Pomerol property on the outskirts of Libourne belongs to a branch of the Moueix family. Claire Moueix left a career in telecommunications to take over from her mother in 2013. In the sandier part of Pomerol, vineyards all around the château are planted with 75% Merlot and 25% Cabernet Franc. The wine ages in one third new oak. Bernard Moueix also owns Château Tauzinat l'Hermitage in St. Emilion .

Château La Tour Figeac

1 La Tour Figeac, BP 007, 33330 St.
Emilion
(33) 05 57 51 77 62
Otto Rettenmaier
latourfigeac@orange.fr

 L'Esquisse de la Tour Figeac

15 ha; 45,000 bottles
[map p. 31]

Figeac is a famous name in St. Emilion, and there are close to a dozen variants in the vicinity of the best known, Château Figeac (many originating in the division of the estate in the late nineteenth century). La Tour Figeac is one of the best. It has been a grand cru classé since 1955. On the plateau of the graves, it has belonged to the Rettenmaier family since 1973: Otto has been in charge since 1990. Vineyards are now 65% Merlot and 35% Cabernet Franc, as the Cabernet Franc has been increased by a program of replanting with selection massale. New oak varies from 60-80% depending on the year.

Château Villemaurine

23 Villemaurine-Sud, 33330 St.
Emilion
(33)0 5 57 74 47 30
Cynthia Capelaere
contact@villemaurine.com
www.villemaurine.com

 Les Angelots de Villemaurine

7 ha; 40,000 bottles
[map p. 31]

Located on the limestone plateau, just to the north outside the walls of St. Emilion, Villemaurine was purchased and renovated in 2007 by Belgian negociant Justin Oncin. Previously it was owned by the negociant Robert Giraud. The wine has improved steadily under its new owner, with vinification now made in a new gravity-feed cuverie. Plantings are 80% Merlot. The second wine comes from specific plots in the vineyard. There is also another wine, Clos Larcis, 100% Merlot from a plot of less than a hectare located between Châteaux Pavie and Larcis-Ducasse.

Château Vrai Canon Bouché

1 Tertre Canon, 33126 Fronsac
(33) 05 57 21 24 68
Jean de Laitre
contact@chateauvraicanonbouche.com
chateauvraicanonbouche.com

In an elevated position in Canon-Fronsac, the vineyards have an atypical terroir based on quarries that were used to provide stone for building Bordeaux. The property changed hands in 1953 and again in 2005 before it was sold in 2014 to LFP Grands Vignobles de France, a subsidiary of a real estate company. A replanting program using selection massale has increased Cabernet Franc to

2 *Le Tertre de Canon*

12 ha; 25,000 bottles
[map p. 28]

30%. The grand vin ages in 50% new barriques. Stéphane Derenoncourt is the consulting wine-maker.

Château Vray Croix de Gay

Siaurac, 33500 Néac
(33) 05 57 51 64 58
Jean Claude Berrouet
info@siaurac.com
www.siaurac.fr

2 *L'Enchanteur*

4 ha; 15,000 bottles
[map p. 30]

This is something of a micro-cuvée, coming from three plots in Pomerol, including one close to Petrus and another close to Trotanoy. Owned by the Guichard family since 1949, the domain was handled by Moueix until Aline Guichard and Paul Goldschmidt took management back into family hands in 2005. In 2014 they sold a large share in their wine estates to François Pinault, owner of Château Latour. The other estates are Château Siau-rac in Lalande de Pomerol and Le Prieuré in St. Emilion. (The wine of Vray Croix de Gay has been made at Siaurac.) Vineyards are 80% Merlot, and the grand vin ages in 50% new barriques. Jean Claude Berrouet, formerly of Petrus, has been con-sulting winemaker since 2014.

Index of Châteaux by Rating

4 star
Château Ausone
Château Cheval Blanc
Petrus

3 star
Château Angélus
Château Canon
Château Canon La Gaffelière
Château La Conseillante
Le Dôme
Château L'Évangile
Château Figeac
Château La Fleur-Pétrus
Château Hosanna
Château Lafleur
Château Latour à Pomerol
La Mondotte
Château Pavie
Le Pin
Château Le Tertre Rôteboeuf
Château Trotanoy
Château Valandraud

2 star
Château Beauséjour Bécot
Château Beauséjour Héritiers
Duffau Lagarrosse
Château Bélair-Monange
Château Bon Pasteur
Château Clinet

Château L'Église Clinet
Clos Fourtet
Château La Gaffelière
Château Gazin
Château Nénin
Château Pavie Macquin
Château Petit Village
Château Roc de Cambes
Château Troplong Mondot
Château Trottevieille
Vieux Château Certan

1 star
Domaine de L'A
Château d'Aiguilhe
Château Beauregard
Château Certan de May
Château La Confession
Château Dassault
Château La Dominique
Château La Fleur de Boüard
Château Fombrauge
Château Fontenil
Château Fougas
Château Le Gay
Château Gombaude Guillot
Château Grand Corbin-Despagne
Château Larcis Ducasse
Château Quintus
Château Rol Valentin

Index of Organic and Biodynamic Châteaux

Domaine de L'A
Château Ampélia
Château Ausone
Château Beauregard
Château Canon La Gaffelière
Clos de L'Oratoire
Clos Puy Arnaud
Château La Conseillante
Château Fonroque
Château Fougas
Château Gombaude Guillot
Gracia
Château Grand Corbin-Despagne
Château Guadet
Château La Croix Taillefer
Château Mazeyres
Château Mondésir-Gazin
La Mondotte
Château Simard
Château Vray Croix de Gay

Index of Châteaux by Appellation

Château Figeac
Château Fleur Cardinale
Château Fombrauge
Château Fonroque
Clos Fourtet
Château Franc Mayne
Château La Gaffelière
Gracia
Château Grand Corbin
Château Grand Corbin-Despagne
Château Grand Mayne
Château Grand Pontet
Château Guadet
Château La Marzelle
Château Larcis Ducasse

Château Monbousquet
La Mondotte
Château Pavie
Château Pavie-Decesse
Château Pavie Macquin
Château Quintus
Château Rol Valentin
Château Simard
Château Soutard
Château Le Tertre Rôteboeuf
Château La Tour Figeac
Château Troplong Mondot
Château Trottevieille
Château Valandraud
Château Villemaurine

Index of Châteaux by Name

Books by Benjamin Lewin MW

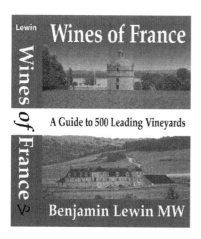

Wines of France

This comprehensive account of the vineyards and wines of France today is extensively illustrated with photographs and maps of each wine-producing area. Leading vineyards and winemakers are profiled in detail, with suggestions for wines to try and vineyards to visit.

Wine Myths and Reality

Extensively illustrated with photographs, maps, and charts, this behind-the-scenes view of winemaking reveals the truth about what goes into a bottle of wine. Its approachable and entertaining style immediately engages the reader in the wine universe.

In Search of Pinot Noir

Pinot Noir is a uniquely challenging grape with an unrivalled ability to reflect the character of the site where it grows. This world wide survey of everywhere Pinot Noir is grown extends from Burgundy to the New World, and profiles leading producers.

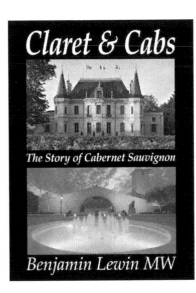

Claret & Cabs: The Story of Cabernet Sauvignon

This worldwide survey of Cabernet Sauvignon and its blends extends from Bordeaux through the New World, defines character of the wine from each region, and profiles leading producers.

88510989R00071

Made in the USA
Middletown, DE
09 September 2018